THE HAPPINESS (R)EVOLUTION

Your hands on, creative guide for eliciting true happiness, authentic success and a lasting sense of peace... from the inside

PAM ELLIS PhD

Cover image: FeaturePics, Pixart

Editing: John MacKinnon and Karen Rought

Canadian Cataloguing First Publication Date: January 2015

ISBN-13: 978-0988008717

KAIZEN INSPIRED LIFE

ISBN-10: 0988008718

Pam Ellis

THE HAPPINESS (R) EVOLUTION

1. Inspirational   2. Overcoming Adversity

3. Self-Help / Personal Growth / Happiness

For all those who have taught me how to see the world through grateful eyes,

You have shown me, through experience, what it means to be truly happy.

I am thankful for you.

TABLE OF CONTENTS

"The only joy in the world is to begin."

-Cesare Pavese

LET'S TALK

"Life is really simple,

but we insist on making it complicated."

-Confucius

The same can be said of true happiness.

WELCOME TO THE HAPPINESS (R)EVOLUTION!

Hello! I'm Pam, the founder of KAIZEN INSPIRED LIFE – Creative Training and Outreach Association and the joyful rabble rouser of the HAPPINESS (R)EVOLUTION.

I'm so glad you've chosen to join me on this wonderful journey of authentic happiness, true success and a greater experience of inner peace than you've ever experienced in the past.

I certainly hope you're ready for the adventure of a lifetime because that, my friend, is precisely what is in store for you!

Before I go any further into what you have to look forward to, I would like to take a quick moment to explain what the name *Kaizen Inspired Life* means.

These three little words in themselves contain an immense amount of life-changing wisdom that, if acted upon, has the power to create some wonderfully positive experiences in your life and in the lives of many.

If something happens to get in your way, and you find that you're not able to complete this book until a later date, you will still have gained a tremendous amount simply by reading this introduction. But that is *only* if you take steps to put this knowledge into practice in your day-to-day living.

KAIZEN: Small steps that disarm fear and lead to continuous improvement through a compounding effect.

INSPIRED: In Spirit, immersed in and filled with the animating essence and energy of life.

LIFE: A moment to moment, creative experience resulting from conscious choices and awareness, which differs greatly from the zombified state, experienced through habitual reactions based on unconscious programs, memories, fears and limiting beliefs.

**Why live life as a re-run program when you can
CREATE something amazing?**

What do you think? How might YOU use these three little words - KAIZEN INSPIRED LIFE - in a personal way to help yourself increase the amount of happiness, true success and inner peace that you experience in your life on a day-to-day basis? Here are a few suggestions that might help spark a few ideas for you.

First, lets take a look at the word **Kaizen.**

At some time or another, most of us have found ourselves playing it safe. Later we secretly wish that we could have the moment back to do it over again in a different way. Sound familiar? Now, imagine how good it might feel if the next time an opportunity came up that held both a benefit for you, along with some fear, you could allow yourself to stop before reacting in a way that you would later regret. Instead of reacting, you would simply notice the fear rising and right there in that special moment, you would become aware of the fact that a pivotal opportunity had been created. Through this increased awareness you would realize you have two choices:

1. You could decide to run away, but if you did, you would be doing so in full awareness by CHOICE, rather than in a REACTIONARY state as you have in the past.

2. You could decide to breathe deeply, relax (even just a little) and CHOOSE to take a tiny step, *any* step, in the direction of a beneficial state.

No matter how small the step was that you chose to take, you would realize you were moving forward rather than backward! You were doing this thing! Even if it were only in the tiniest, teensiest way, you would still be doing much more than you had before! You would be facing your fear, and winning this time.

No regrets baby!

Through this successful step, you could see how easy it is to create change. And the best part is... You would know, without a doubt, that you could do this again and again.

It's really not necessary to become some fearless adrenaline junkie, bounding through life with one enormous, innovative leap after another in order to create success. Remember the meaning of Kaizen: *small steps* that disarm fear and lead us to continuous improvement through a compounding effect, like a snowball rolling down a hill, building in size through the use of natural momentum. The truth is that even the tiniest micro-mini-baby-steps that we take on a progressive basis will get us to where we're going *much* faster than any of the grandest intentions that scare the daylights out of us and keep us stuck in the land of procrastination and regrets.

Now, let's take a look at the word **inspired.**

We all know that there is so much more to life than that which meets the eye. The question is, how much are we willing to acknowledge, personally? Synchronicity, intuition, a nudge to turn left instead of right, helpful people that show up at the perfect time, along with the person that calls us just as we're thinking of them... how do we account for all this? How many of us even try to understand this? How many of these moments are we actually paying attention to? How aware are we? Paying attention requires a little effort on our parts along with the desire to stop and take notice in order to create change.

This brings us to the million dollar question: Are we willing to put in the effort that it takes to use this inspired energy in a conscious way? Thankfully this does not need to be a difficult thing. Here again, we can apply the philosophy of Kaizen small steps. There is absolutely no need to become a super hero mega-guru overnight. Truthfully, no one could stand to be around you if you did. How about just beginning to explore these little everyday miracles with a little more wonder, a little more awe, and a little more interest and awareness? You might even like to start tomorrow. *Carpe diem*, as they say! When you wake up in the morning and your feet hit the floor, say to yourself...

"I wonder what **wonderful** *things life has in store for me today?"*

By digging a little deeper into your experiences, with even the tiniest bit of **curiosity**, instead of just skimming the surface of your perceived sense of "reality" and missing all of the **interesting** things, you will discover a new depth to LIFE in so many ways. Doesn't that sound **exciting**?

Next, let's look at the word **life**.

Here again, we face the question: Are we *choosing* our actions based on the current moment and what is actually happening, or are we REacting to the experience based on what we feel has "always" been?

The truth is, life can only be experienced in the here and now, not in the regrets of the past or the worries about tomorrow. If you only had this one moment, here and now, what would you do differently?

About five years ago, the following quote from Lao Tzu just happened to fall into my hands at the perfect time. It was right at a time when I was about to make a major life change. Just before receiving this quote I was feeling the pressure of my situation.

After the breakup of my marriage of twenty three years, I was about to leave my home and begin a new life with my three young children. As you might imagine, fear was lurking pretty close to me; nipping at my heels on a daily basis. I needed some inspiration BIG TIME, and here it was in my hands. Immediately I recognized these words as **truth,** and as a result I made the change that I needed to make with far more grace and ease than I would have otherwise. When it comes to TRULY LIVING, the following quote says it all for me.

"If you are depressed, you are living in the past.

If you are anxious, you are living in the future.

If you are at peace, you are living in the present."

Another everyday miracle, wouldn't you say?

．　　　．　　　．

The next thing I'd like to do before diving into things is to take a moment to point out to you how this book is laid out. As a working parent with young kids, I completely understand how stretched most of us are feeling, time wise. So in the Spirit of Kaizen small steps, I've created a way for everyone to make use of this book, no matter how busy their life may be. As you flip through the pages, you'll notice that the chapters are divided into three parts:

Part 1. Kaizenized Quick Notes

Part 2. The Extended Version

Part 3. Creative Exploration.

In the first part, the Kaizenized Quick Notes *summarize the main points that will be covered in each chapter. Reading these quickly can be helpful in a few ways:*

1.   If you're feeling a little pressed for time, and would like to experience what this book has to offer very quickly, you can simply skim through these notes. Taking one chapter at a time, you can easily tap into the bits of gold that I've left for you. If you act upon these hints, you will definitely enrich your life in many wonderful ways.

2.   If you would like to make the most of this book by taking it slowly (which is highly recommended, by the way), you can read these quick notes before delving into the extended version. By doing so, your mind will be focusing more clearly on the points... your subconscious will be alert, looking for these points in the writing. Used in this way, the Kaizen Quick notes are like little appetizers for the brain, making it hungry for the main course.

3.   If, after reading this book fully, you would like a quick refresher of the main points covered, you can skim through the quick notes and instantly find yourself inspired again as you reconnect with the wisdom and techniques once again.

In a nutshell, the Kaizenized Quick Notes can help you to take the pressure off the process if necessary, while you continue to benefit from the experience. This feature can be beneficial when it come to making the most of your time, especially in those moments when life gets extremely busy.

The second part of each chapter is called the **Extended Version**. Here, the key points will be explored in greater depth. Even though it is clearly much quicker and easier to skim the Kaizenized Quick Notes, please be aware that it is definitely in your best interest to read the entire book at least once, preferably more. There is a wealth of information to draw upon, and a second or third read can often reveal things the mind skipped (or forgot) the first time around.

The third part of each chapter is the fun part! I think you're going to like it most of all. This is where the real gold is! In the **Creative Exploration** section, you will have the opportunity to experiment with the information from each chapter in a hands-on way. Even though you will find a few techniques and exercises sprinkled through the extended version as well, it is the creative exploration section where you will *really* be able to prove to yourself that this process works! Best of all, you'll see how enjoyable it can be to easily add more happiness, true success and inner peace to your life.

What better way is there to learn and understand anything than to put it to the test by *using* it personally? In fact, for most people, this is the *only* way to truly learn something. As an example, I share the following scenario with my students. It clearly illustrates the absolute need for *experiential* learning.

Imagine for a moment that you would like to learn how to fly a plane. You might read books about flying. You might learn all of the intricate, detailed mechanics involved in flying. You might listen to people who tell you how good it feels to fly, how enjoyable the experience is and how much they love the freedom it provides. You might have all the information you could ever want about all the different types of planes on the market. You have learned how to fly in theory. You may even go out and reserve a plane for the day, but tell me, if you jumped into the cockpit right now and started the engine, what would happen? Chances are, you'd realize pretty quickly that you really don't know *how* to fly at all! Everything is much different in theory than it is when it comes right down to practical experience.

Only by practicing, by getting yourself in that plane and flying (hopefully with an instructor), will you ever really learn *how* to fly experientially. Even when you do learn, it takes time for the process to become second nature. This happens only through practice.

The same goes for the process of *learning* how to be happy, to be truly successful and to consciously choose to be at peace. In this experience, as with any other, practice makes all the difference.

You can read a thousand books, listen to a thousand CDs and learn as much as you want in theory about happiness, but until you choose to get into your own plane on the path to self-mastery, you will never really understand the depth of what it means to fly. You will never really know what this or any other process can provide you experientially.

This being said, I also want to acknowledge the importance of reading, studying and understanding in theory. It, too, is a positive part of the process. But without the action, there can be no lasting change.

Tell me and I forget.

Teach me and I may remember.

Involve me and I learn."

—Benjamin Franklin

Finally, before we begin, I'd like to cover one more crucial detail. The information that I am about to share with you here was not pulled out of thin air, but rather it came as a result of hands on experience in my own life – hard earned experience in fact. You see, even though right now I might be known as the "Happiness Chick," I wasn't always. My life certainly has not been without some incredible challenges.

You have most likely heard the saying, "Necessity is the mother of all invention." Well, I must admit to you that the "HAPPINESS (R)"EVOLUTION" falls into this category perfectly. In fact, this book could easily be described as the result of one very painful, fall flat on my face, get back up again, fly around the world by the seat of my pants journey.

In order to give you an idea of what I mean by this, I'd like to offer you a little glimpse into what my life looked like before I discovered the techniques that I'm about to share with you in this book. Within the span of five short years, I experienced the following, among many other things...

In the midst of my third battle with postpartum depression, my Dad was diagnosed with esophageal cancer. After numerous surgeries, and various forms of treatment over a three year span, he succumbed to this horrible disease and passed away while I sat by his bed, holding his hand.

Approximately a year into his struggle, my Mother in law, who was also my art mentor and one of my dearest friends, became sick as well. She was diagnosed with ALS and died less than a year before my Dad.

In the process of dealing with the depression while suffering from the grief of both my father's and mother's illnesses and deaths, I too was experiencing my own serious physical challenges. Three months before my Dad's death, I discovered a lump in my breast. Then two weeks before his funeral I landed myself in a wheelchair. After four months, unable to walk due to an accident, my marriage fell apart. As a result I chose to leave my family home with my kids.

You would think that this would be enough to bring a person to their knees. Well, it did. But it didn't stop there... What followed soon knocked me off my knees and right onto my seat.

Being on my own in a new place, I had no one near that I could call upon for help when things went wrong and sure enough, they did. The first week that I moved in, the stove broke, which was soon followed by the dishwasher. Thankfully, with the help of a Facebook friend talking me through the repair process step by step, I managed to fix both appliances myself! But that was just the beginning of the challenges this house would bring to me...

Next came the water main that burst not one time, or two, but THREE times within the course of a year. Two of those times the break was on my side of the property line, which made it my responsibility to fix. With one challenge landing in my lap after the next, along with very little money and even less help, I soon discovered that I had two choices:

1. Be miserable and in the process make my kids miserable too. Or...

2. Find a way to move through these experiences with a little grace, while focusing on ways to bring more happiness into my life for the sake of both myself and that of my kids.

The good news is, I chose the latter, and here I am today, standing taller than ever before with a smile on my face. Thanks to the challenges that I faced I was able to discover the truth about happiness including what it is, and how to elicit the experience of this state through natural means, no matter what is happening in life externally. Now, as a result, I am sharing what I have learned in the hopes that you too can move through your own life challenges with greater ease while experiencing far more happiness, success and inner peace.

As you can see, the HAPPINESS (R)EVOLUTION most definitely came about as a result of my own need to escape misery. But the challenges that I shared with you above only reflect a turning point in my life. The truth is, the real unhappiness began many years earlier, when I was a young child.

Before the HAPPINESS (R)EVOLUTION journey began, I didn't have a clue about what it actually meant to be *truly* happy. To be fair, how could I? Happiness wasn't something that was taught by anyone when I was growing up. You just got on with life. That's just the way it was. So, like many others, I simply based my sense of happiness, success and inner peace on everything outside of me. I figured that if I had what I wanted and things were going well, I was happy. What a huge mistake that was!

Trying, searching, striving, and constantly questioning myself every step of the way, it always felt as though I was coming up short. No matter what I did, the critical voice inside my head made darn sure that I never felt quite good enough, never felt smart enough or witty enough, welcome enough, thin enough, talented enough, rich enough, or successful enough. I always felt myself needing to strive for more and more in order to earn my way to happiness. But no matter how hard I tried, I never felt worthy.

Along with the demanding inner voice, the critical eyes and ears of perfectionism made it nearly impossible to accept any type of compliment for all of my hard work and striving. Yet, ironically, this same perfectionism drove me to constantly seek outer confirmation in order to convince myself that I was on the right track and doing the right thing in the right way. Like an addict, however, no matter how much outer confirmation I received, I could never seem to get enough to satisfy my growing needs and dependency. I always needed another fix.

After a while, I came to the conclusion that happiness was something I would have to wait for. But how long would I have to wait? It already felt like an eternity. I thought that maybe happiness might come when I could finally reach my goals. But sadly, it didn't. Instead there were just more and more goals that showed up in its place.

Then, one day, a critical point was reached, the point of no return when I could no longer stand to live the life that I was living, in the way that I was living it. I didn't know what to look for, or what I would find, but I just knew that I *had* to step out of the box that I had created for myself and find a better way. Something had to give. I needed a change in a big way.

At that moment, it became crystal clear that if I ever wanted to experience *true* happiness for any longer than a fleeting moment, I would have to begin by UNlearning a lot of things. I sensed that it wasn't going to be easy, or pretty. But, even so, I was ready. By this point I wanted true happiness more than ANYTHING, and I was ready to do whatever it took to get it.

So now, I ask you, does any part of this story sound familiar to you? If so, you've got to know right now that you are in good company. There are many of us who have been wanting the same thing. When it comes right down to it, though, who doesn't crave true happiness? Who walks around saying, 'Nope not me, no happiness for me, thanks. I prefer to live in misery.'

Well, maybe there are a few people out there like that. But thankfully you are not one of them. And the good news is that after reading this book, you will be walking away with some powerful techniques you can use again and again, on a daily basis, to continue to increase the depth and quality of true happiness in your life. Remember, no matter how good it gets, there is always another step to take.

Thankfully, what I learned on my journey is that it's not difficult to choose to be happy, when you know how, that is. The truth is, it's very easy. Being miserable is *much* harder to maintain. It's much more stressful and far more draining.

HAPPINESS, on the other hand, is the most natural state to BE.

We've simply been programmed by society to believe that it's hard to find lasting happiness. We have been led to believe that our happiness is dependent on particular things. Thanks to some pretty clever advertising and other forms of media, we have bought into the belief that in order to feel happy we need particular things to fall into place or into our laps, whatever the case may be.

I'm here today to kick this myth to the curb and SHOW you first hand that this is NOT the case. In the pages to follow I will PROVE to you that there is a simple way to experience true happiness regardless of the circumstances in your life, regardless of what you have or have not, and no matter what you feel you may still want or need.

As you move through this book, you will be provided with an opportunity to follow a simple, creative method for producing happiness at will. In the process you will be presented with a variety of well tested techniques designed to help you to make the most of your journey in a way that results in a greater depth of joy, authentic success and inner peace on a daily basis. You will also discover the ten essential elements that are necessary in the creation a happy life.

Sound good? Well, buckle up because it gets even better.

The good news is this: You cannot have true happiness without also experiencing the added bonus of increased relaxation and creativity. Now, at this point I'm guessing you would like to dive right in. I don't blame you! In fact, I feel the same! However, before we get to the gold, I would like to share a few valuable tips on how you can make the most of this journey:

First of all... CELEBRATE!

Historically, the beginning of any life-enhancing journey has been a cause for joy and celebration. I'd say the journey into true happiness certainly qualifies here!

Taking Kaizen small steps into mind, there is no need to make this celebration elaborate, costly or time consuming. In fact, the simplest rituals can often have the greatest impact on the heart and mind.

Any of the following activities can prove to be profoundly significant celebrations and are often worth far more than any expensive dinner or shopping spree could ever be.

- *Lighting a candle*
- *Arranging some flowers*
- *Taking a walk in a beautiful place*

The trick to making your celebration special is simply to allow yourself to fully engage in the process. Pay attention, be present and enjoy the experience.

DOCUMENT YOUR JOURNEY!

I highly recommend that you go out right now and get yourself a special journal that you will use exclusively for this journey. In fact, how about buying a copy of the HAPPINESS (R)EVOLUTION CREATIVE EXPLORATION JOURNAL? You can find it on Amazon, or through our webpage: KaizenInspiredLife.com/books/

Carefully designed to complement the HAPPINESS (R)EVOLUTION guidebook; this unique 8.5" x 11" creative exploration journal contains over 495 pages of inspiration, including:

- 12 months of enjoyable, awareness raising exercises that coordinate month by month with the specific HAPPINESS (R)EVOLUTION's elements for creating more joy, authentic success and inner peace,
- 52 weeks of encouraging quotes and passages,
- 365 days worth of affirmative messages
- Room to write your own personal notes,
- Pages to doodle, draw, collage, vision board, document and explore your journey in your own unique way.

Of course any journal can be used in this process, but why not take advantage of this pure creative gold that is available to you?

You also might like to pick up a special pen you put aside and use exclusively in your HAPPINESS journal. Make sure it feels good in your hand and that it's pleasing to your eye as well. By taking quick notes along the way, you can clearly see the progression of your journey in a way that can help you, not only today, but in the coming years as well. You will also be able to witness how your experience is creating changes for you, and you will notice how far you have come. Without a written account, it is far too easy to sweep your progress under the rug and forget where you were when you began. I have seen it in myself and others. Writing does make a difference.

I recommend scheduling a few minutes each day to read, write and explore this process on a steady basis, rather than trying to cram it all in over the course of a few days. And I do mean schedule. If you don't set aside the time, by physically entering it into your calendar, it will be far too easy for you to miss a day. One day will then lead to two, and then to three, and eventually the process will just slip away entirely. This problem, however, can be easily avoided with a little proactive measure: schedule it.

How about taking a moment right here and now to "pencil in" even five minutes a day for you? Yes, you read that right. I did say *five* minutes. There's no rush to do more. It's not a race. In fact, this is a journey that will last a lifetime as you continue to explore even greater depths of happiness. Why would you want to rush yourself when you can savor each precious moment?

And finally, if you would like to take things even deeper still, feel free to join Kaizen Inspired Life's Happiness (R)Evolution group either in person or online. You can check it out and register by visiting our website: KaizenInspiredLife.com

By joining this group, you will not only delve deeper into the techniques and learn much more in an experiential way, but you will also be connecting with other like-minded individuals who are on a similar journey.

And now that we've taken care of all the background and housekeeping...

Grab yourself a cup of tea or java.

Make yourself comfy, and...

Let's BEGIN!

HAPPINESS

"Happiness is the meaning and the purpose of life, the whole aim and end of human existence."

Aristotle

Kaizenized Quick Notes

- *Happiness is a state of being rather than an emotion, as many people currently believe.*

- *True happiness encompasses a variety of emotions.*

- *Happiness is not dependent on any external factors. It is an inside job... entirely.*

- *The majority of people today believe they will be happy when the pieces of their life fall into place. However, it is the opposite that is true. By choosing to elicit happiness in the current moment, regardless of what is happening, life naturally begins to improve on all levels: physically, materially, emotionally, mentally, psychologically and spiritually as well.*

- *Happy people are naturally successful. However, their success may not always appear in the way that we, as a society, "think" it should be. Regardless, success does come in an ideal way for the individual, personally. The best part about this kind of authentic success is that it occurs in an easy, natural and deeply fulfilling way.*

- *Through the method presented in this book you can and will experience far greater depths of happiness, true success and lasting inner peace in every area of your life.*

But there is one catch: this process cannot simply be read about; it must be experienced through action as a hands-on, creative journey. By choosing to actively engage in the techniques you will begin to see, feel and experience positive changes taking place in your life immediately.

The Extended Version

Do you know what true happiness is?

A great place to begin this journey is by taking a look at what happiness *is not.* Does that surprise you a little? Actually, I hope it surprises you a lot. Part of this method involves the art of letting go. By setting aside (even for a moment) the way we *think* things *should* be, we create the conditions that allow **truth** to shine through freely.

Just as the parting of dark clouds on a stormy day reveals the brilliant light and warmth of the sun, so too will you find that working with contrast, or the opposite in the form of *"is not"* in this capacity, has the power to reveal what *"is" in* the most beautiful, life enhancing way. As you read the list of "is nots" below, please draw your attention to how these ideas make you feel. Check off the points that catch your attention more than others, and then ask yourself what might be causing you to feel this way about this particular point. What does it remind you of in your own life? A little journaling here can be helpful.

Please note: The more open and honest you can be with yourself, resisting the urge to sugar-coat anything, the more happiness you will experience as a result.

True Happiness...

- ☐ Is NOT dependent on having a certain amount of money in your wallet or in the bank.

- ☐ Is NOT based on where you live, what car you drive, or what your home looks like, inside or out.

- ☐ Is NOT based on whether or not you have physical freedom, or even good health.

- ☐ Is definitely NOT dependent on the toys you own, the clothes you wear or the company you keep.

- ☐ In fact, it is NOT dependent on any external factor at all.

- ☐ It also does not mean you will no longer feel sadness, grief or pain. (You *can* feel happiness in spite of all these.)

- ☐ It does not require that you repress or suppress anything you are currently feeling, experiencing or remembering.

- ☐ It is not achieved through force in any way. It cannot be coerced, or manipulated through guilt, shame, denial or will power.

- ☐ No one and nothing has the power to make you feel it, nor does anyone or anything have the power to take it away from you.

- ☐ In fact, true happiness has never left you, no matter how long it has been since you felt it last.

Of course, there are many more myths and misconceptions

surrounding true happiness. As you were reading through the list, did you notice any others that came to mind for you? Please feel free to write them down in your journal.

"Your task is not to seek for love, but merely to seek and find all the barriers within yourself that you have built against it."

—Rumi

The same can be said for happiness as well.

Now that we have looked at what happiness is not, let's take a moment to explore what it *might* be.

What I have found most interesting in my own happiness quest and the research that has surrounded it, is that although it can be fairly easy for people to agree on what happiness is *not*, it is not always as easy for them to agree on what it *is*. It seems that when it comes to true happiness, one size does not fit all, and a clear description, that all can agree upon, is very tricky to create.

I remember a few years back, I asked a client to describe what she was hoping to experience in her life. We talked about what she truly wanted to feel. I was expecting, of course, for her to say "happy," as most people did. But to my surprise she did not say this.

Instead, she looked me straight in the eye without wavering and said, *"I don't really need to feel happy. What I need is to feel comfortable, content and safe."* Her words stayed with me for a very long time. They gave me much to contemplate.

In my experience, I would have described authentic happiness as having all of the qualities my client mentioned above, yet when I proposed this suggestion to her at the time, she adamantly stated that these descriptions were *not* the same at all. After further contemplation and exploration, however, it became clear that this client was experiencing a fear associated with the word *happiness*. If she allowed herself to *want* happiness she would also be allowing herself to feel the opposite as well. She was afraid of being disappointed if happiness did not come. For her, the chance of disappointment was far too high a price to pay. It was safer for her to use words other than happiness... yet the essence that she was seeking was still one and the same. The truth is it doesn't really matter what you call it, as long as you feel it. Isn't that what really counts anyway?

Happiness is a state of consciousness.

It is our true, natural, unfettered state of being, which no one has the power to give to us and therefore no one has the power to take it away...

It needs only to be accessed in order to be experienced

There is no such thing as a grey sky

Just as the clouds cannot stop the sun from shining, no matter how rainy it may be, there is also no outer condition in life that ever has the power to take away our happiness, but this is true only if we choose to see it this way. Even though it may be temporarily hidden from our awareness in the storms of life, happiness is always here, present within us. It has always existed just under the surface, waiting for the clouds to part so that it might shine through our lives again.

In this book you will have the opportunity to gain powerful techniques that can make it easier to reach right in and part those clouds yourself, and you will be able to do it consciously, at will. Sound interesting? Can you imagine what that might look like and how good that might feel?

By simply using our imagination along with our memories, we allow ourselves to remember who and what we are in the deepest sense. When we do, the clouds can and will, naturally recede and the sun's light, our own light, will shine through once again.

One of the quickest and easiest ways to do this is by noticing how much we have to be grateful for in this current moment.

Happiness -- our true state of being -- and gratitude go hand and hand. It's impossible to have one without the other.

Tell me, when was the last time *you* were grateful without feeling a measure of happiness? To take it one step further: The last time you were truly happy, were you not also grateful for this state and this feeling as well?

Are you ready to get your happy on today?

When I say to you that no one and no thing has the power to make you happy or to keep you from being happy, do you believe me? Here's a better question still: Do you KNOW this to be true, through your own experiences? Be honest with yourself now. Remember, there is no place for sugar coating or denial in this process. Is it possible that somewhere inside yourself there could be a small voice that might be saying any of the following things:

- If only you knew what I was going through. It's just so hard to be happy when all of this stuff is happening.

- He hurt me, she hurt me. If they wouldn't have done that I know I would still be happy.

- This situation is so hard. No one understands.

- If only I had enough money, enough time, enough love in my life; that would make it so much easier.

- If only I had what I need, then I could be happy!

If any of the statements above sound familiar, please know you are not alone. There is definitely no shame in feeling this way. At some point in time each one of us has said at least one of those things. In fact, I've personally said ALL of them *many* times in the past, and at times… even when I knew better.

Nope, no shame and no regrets. They're not helpful anyway. Besides, this is just part of the human state of consciousness. It's not the end of the world to feel this way and I guarantee that eventually we will all evolve beyond these feelings, and we will do so in a natural, creative and progressive way. But for now let's just focus on taking small steps and celebrating each small success along the way. This will get us much further in the long run.

Along with small steps and celebrating success, it can be helpful to understand that the statements above merely reflect our natural instinct for self preservation in this lifetime. Often this impulse can result in feeling the need to place the blame for our unhappiness on someone else or something else. This is especially true when we believe that the experiences in our life are happening "to" us as a result of some outside force. But let me ask you this: If you *knew* that things were not, in fact, happening "to" you but rather "for" you, for a greater purpose, how might you see things differently? It's amazing what a shift in perception like this can create. By acknowledging the possibility that life might be working in our favor, no matter what the external situation looks like, we gain the ability to release resistance within ourselves. In turn we create the necessary conditions (again, within ourselves) that allow us to throw open the doors to true happiness and in turn encourage joy to flow right in.

This particular shift in perception happened *for* me in the year 2000. I had recently separated from my husband. My two year old son and I lived together in a little house on the corner of a busy street. As a single mother, money was very tight, and so was time. No matter how hard I worked, it always felt as though I needed to work harder in order to earn enough just to get by. At the same time, however, I also felt that I needed to spend more time with my son. We were always on the go, hurrying to daycare and hurrying off to work. Then it was pickup time and back home for dinner then off to bed. Needless to say, this was a challenging time. Feeling my heart and attention torn in so many directions, there was little time or energy for myself or the things I wanted to do, including spending time with my son. Happiness felt like it had hit an all time low. I must admit, nothing at this point in my life really felt like it was working "*for*" us, but it sure as heck felt as though there was a LOT working against us or "*to*" us.

Then one drizzly November morning something incredible happened that changed my perspective in a BIG way. While trying to get from the house to the car without becoming completely soaked, I felt a tug on my arm. My son all of a sudden decided to stop in his tracks. As the rain poured down even harder, he began yelling excitedly, *"Look! Look Mommy!"*

Pointing off into the distance, waving his arm wildly, Mr. Stubborn Pants refused to budge from his spot until I looked at what he was trying to show me. Feeling a cold trickle of water rolling down my neck, I shivered and felt myself sink a little. *"Oh no, not today!* I thought. But thankfully before I could say anything out loud, my little boy piped up again. This time he was squealing with delight. He said to me, *"I LOOOOVE blue skies, Mommy!"*

Getting wetter by the second, and running late *again*, my patience was wearing pretty thin. *Are you freakin' kidding me?* I thought. *What BLUE sky? It's pouring, kid!* Once again, very thankful for the fact that this thought did not have the chance to develop into speech, I gave in and looked up to see what he was pointing at. In that split second of letting go and letting be, the world stood still.

No longer did it matter how wet we were. No longer did it matter how late we would be. In fact, nothing mattered anymore except the exact moment I was experiencing with my son. And what an experience it was! Right there in front of us was the most beautiful sight that either of us had ever seen. Amidst the blackest of clouds, the most glorious patch of blue sky began to appear. But that wasn't all. As the clouds continued to part even further, the sun's rays burst through and began to pour down with the rain. My heart jumped up as tears began to fall. The sight touched my heart beyond words. In fact, as I write this now, the tears once again are welling up in my eyes as my heart is being touched again. Then at once I remembered something. Now it was my turn to wave my arms in the air, and tell my son to look!

Do you recall what happens when you turn around and face your back to the sun while it's shining on a rainy day? That's right, and there it was in all its glory, the most incredibly vibrant rainbow, right in front of our eyes! And the best part of all is that we got to share it together that day.

In that moment I realized a profound truth that would touch my life from that point forward: without the challenge, in this case the rain, and my son's stubborn streak, we would never have had the precious opportunity to experience such beauty on that grey November day. We would have hurried right by in our typical morning rush. We would have missed the treasure that was right there for all to see. In fact, I wondered at the time how many moments like that had occurred in the past without us noticing. But never mind that. The past has passed and thankfully we always have another opportunity to stop and begin again. That morning was a beginning for me. Just as the sky opened, so did my heart and mind. All at once I knew there was no such thing as a grey sky, only grey clouds, and they were only temporary. I also knew that without the contrast of the rain and the darkness, we could never experience the beauty, the color and the amazing light we saw that day.

To add to the list of happy blessings we both received from this experience, was a game we created together as a result of our *blue sky day*.

At that time I was learning about the law of attraction and the power of intention. Together, my son and I began our own experiment with these concepts and we did so in our own simple way. Each cloudy day we would both fill our hearts with as much love as we could, then each of us would repeat three times...

"I LOVE BLUE SKY!   I LOVE BLUE SKY!   I LOOOOOVE BLUE SKY!"

Next, we would look around, scanning the clouds to see what we could see. Sure enough, every time we looked, there it was before our eyes: a little patch of blue somewhere in the sky. At times it would be a large patch of blue, while other times just a little speck. But regardless of the size, it was *always* there, reminding us that there is no such thing as a grey sky.

Please feel free to try this little game yourself, if you'd like. This is just one of the *many* simple, creative ways to prove to yourself there is *always* another way to see things.

A shift in attitude, perception and perspective can go a very long way on the road to true happiness.

In the following chapters we'll be exploring many more simple, yet creative techniques like this that can make it far easier for you to part the clouds within your own state of mind, no matter where you are, and no matter what you might be facing in life... rain or shine.

To help you feel a little more at ease and confident that you too can make this work for you, I would like to assure you that everything I offer to you here, in this book, I have tested on myself over and over again. These techniques and viewpoints are not simply book-learned theory. They are games I've played, techniques I've put to use, and tools that have made a profound difference in my life and in the lives of my clients and students as well. And I can say to you with absolute confidence that they *can* have a profound effect on *your* life as well, but only if you put them to use.

In the same breath, however, I would also like to make it clear that I do not guarantee that by reading this book you will no longer have challenges in your life. I do not guarantee that suddenly all your dreams will materialize *automatically*... although they might. But, what I do guarantee is this: if you follow along, step by step and put this information into practice on a daily basis, you *will* discover the authentic essence of happiness within yourself. You will learn how to access this happiness, even in the most challenging times, and in the process you will begin to see, feel and notice wonderful changes taking place in *all* aspects of your life. Along with eliciting happiness, you will also begin to notice an increase in your natural ability to relax at will, with far greater ease. Now, really, what more could you ask for? Something coming to mind? Go ahead and ask! When you have happiness flowing through you freely, you'll be amazed at what you can accomplish. Asking is part of that journey, by the way.

One more thing: an additional bonus you will receive on this journey of happiness and gratitude is a compilation of the key elements required to naturally access the wealth of creative resources, hidden talents and abilities that exist within yourself. So, if you are one who claims not to have one creative bone in your body, you will soon come to know that you're right! You do *not* have ONE creative bone, but rather you have many! And if you already feel that you are fairly well off in the creativity department, the good news is you are about to discover the fact that your creative treasure chest is far deeper than you ever could have dreamed possible. In this case you too are in for a wonderful treat!

Creative Exploration

Please take a moment now to pull out your happiness journal and your special pen. Give yourself a few minutes to explore the following questions. As you do, jot down some quick notes of the things that come to mind. Once this is complete, simply relax and allow these exercises to continue to sit in the back of your mind as food for thought or contemplation that you can carry with you for the rest of the day.

Please feel free to bring your journal with you as you move through this journey and feel free to continue to write down quick thoughts and feelings when you feel drawn to do so, no matter whether its just a word here or there, or even a sentence or two per day. Every little bit that you add to this process will help you to make the most of this journey.

1. How would YOU personally describe happiness?

Write a list of at least FIVE descriptive words or phrases that accurately define the feeling you would like to experience. In other words, describe what true happiness means to you.

For example, you might choose to use the words **joyfulness**, **inner peace**, **safety**, **giddiness**, a **bubbly tummy** or even the feeling of **love** and **connecting with your essential self** as some of your descriptions. If five minutes is easy for you, how about trying 10 or maybe even 20?

Hint: Recalling times in the past when you have felt happiness can make this exercise much easier to do.

Next, ask yourself where in your life you are experiencing this feeling already, even just a little bit.

Is there a way that you can expand upon this feeling? Is there something that you can do to help make this feeling grow a little more? This can be as simple as paying attention to it when it occurs.

2. Give yourself permission to pay attention to everyday miracles and synchronicity.

I encourage you to take your time while reading this book. You might like to spread it out over the course of a few weeks or even a month. During this time, I encourage you to savor each bit of information, play with each exercise, and experiment with the concepts. See how each of them apply to your own life and experience.

While you do this I also recommend that you allow yourself to heighten your level of awareness a tiny bit. Pay attention to the little things in your life. Allow yourself to become a little more interested in the simple things that are often missed in the course of a busy day. Keep your eyes and ears open a little more. Expect to notice many more things "pop out" for you and catch your attention over the next while, such as colors becoming brighter, sounds becoming clearer, and your feelings and intuition becoming a little more perceptible.

When you do notice something that catches your attention, quickly jot down a short note in your journal. Be sure to take a few seconds to do this, even if you honestly believe that you will remember the experience in detail. It is important not put too much faith in memory at this point. Just as dreams often have the tendency to slip out of memory upon waking, so too can these little miracles slip away from our memory when life gets in the way and distracts us with something that it deems "more important."

By simply taking a moment to write down a word or two, you will find it far easier to recall these little miracles any time you would like to.

If, however, you simply cannot bring yourself to write notes, you might like to explore some other ways that can make it possible for you to keep track of your experiences. Digital recorders can work wonders for those who do not like to write.

Taking photographs with your phone can also provide helpful reminders. What else might you do to help yourself remember these everyday miracles?

3. What does your blue sky look like?

What symbol might serve to remind you that happiness is always within reach? What might help you to remember that it is always there, right beneath the surface, waiting to be activated?

What particular sign might help you to remember your intention throughout the day, especially when the clouds roll in and life becomes a little more challenging?

Your own personal symbol can be anything that catches your attention and lifts your heart in a way that naturally induces happiness in the moment

It is only possible to live happily ever after

on a day to day basis.

Margaret Bonnano

R...   RELAXATION

Plenty of people miss their share of happiness, not because they never found it, but because they didn't stop to enjoy it.

-- William Feather

Kaizenized Quick Notes

- *Relaxation improves our ability to experience happiness, true success and inner peace. Without a measure of relaxation, we experience restriction, tension and stress in a way that does not allow us to feel true happiness or lasting inner peace in the way we would like to. The good news is it only takes the slightest increase of relaxation to create a profound effect on our ability to access happiness in the moment.*

- *When the Amygdala (the fear center in the brain) is triggered through the feeling of discomfort, the mind immediately blocks our access to focused thought and creativity. This is experienced for each of us in varying degrees, depending on the situation we are in. Within this reactive state, we are disconnected from our natural ability to experience happiness. Relaxation disarms the Amygdala, which diffuses fear and naturally allows happiness to flow through our experiences with ease once again.*

- *Relaxation also opens the channel to our innate creative resources, which results in many beneficial changes to our lives. It does so predominately by showing us that we always have a choice.*

- *True (unforced) creativity is a powerful way to elicit*

relaxation. This type of creativity can be as simple as "creating" a conscious breath in full awareness.

- *There are various techniques (some of which are listed in the creative exploration section of this chapter) that can help us to disarm the Amygdala in an easy way, thereby reconnecting us with creativity, focused thought and choice, all of which have the ability to help us to experience even greater depths of true happiness, success and inner peace.*

The Extended Version

What is relaxation, really?

Most people believe that relaxation is experienced predominantly on a physical level, but in truth, it runs much deeper than this. Like happiness, true relaxation begins in the mind as a choice. It is a richer experience than we give it credit for in which we allow ourselves to be fully present in any particular moment without judgment, and without forcing our will.

As we allow ourselves to relax, we find that we are better able to trust in the process of life, and in the natural unfoldment of our current circumstances. By releasing our need to control the current situation, we also let go of stress, resistance and tension on many levels: physically, emotionally and mentally. This "letting go" in turn creates favorable conditions that allow our experiences to develop naturally in the best way possible for all concerned.

Some may call this a letting go of the ego. Others may say they are letting God control their destiny. I call it a process of releasing the hold that fear has on us, while in turn allowing the best to be.

Let go and let be

True relaxation diminishes worry and stress, while it opens our hearts and minds to something greater than that which appears to be the obvious. It opens us up to something greater than our fears, and reveals to us something far grander than that which has always been. When it comes down to it, haven't we all had enough of re-run programming in our lives? Isn't it time for each of us to create something new?

During the state of true relaxation, we become pure open channels in which creativity, resourcefulness, and wisdom can flow through freely. The result of this relaxation and openness is a sense of freedom, pure happiness and inner peace.

Unfortunately, when we don't consciously understand what is happening or how we achieved this happy state, we often believe that it's uncontrollable and fleeting. Because of this instability, it is also natural to find ourselves laying credit to something outside of ourselves; we believe something or someone *made* us happy. This belief, however, is a dangerous one in that it places us in the position of being a victim of life, rather than a creator. We give away our power to other people and other things in the hope that they will continue to make us happy.

Talk about pressure for everyone involved!

Like a rollercoaster ride, in this state we can easily find ourselves experiencing extreme highs and lows. We feel vulnerable, and at the mercy of the twists and turns that are handed to us by life and by others, while others in turn feel resentful for the position we've placed them in. And the cycle continues. Here we go 'round again.

43

As soon as our happiness begins to slip away, and we begin to allow fear to creep in, the channel within ourselves begins to close tighter once again. We become restricted, and life becomes more difficult, less enjoyable and far more stressful. In effect, we become UNhappy. That's just no fun for anyone!

The Amygdala

The Amygdala, (*pronounced uh*-mig-*duh-luh*), also known as the fear center within the brain, is a small almond-shaped structure located deep within the temporal lobe. The Amygdala's main function is to process strong emotions such as fear, anger and anxiety.

The Amygdala is triggered by the feeling of discomfort in a way that indicates a possible threat to our state of well being on any level. This could happen through experiences such as:

- coming face to face with a tiger in the jungle

- waiting for your turn to give a talk in front of the class

- being placed on the spot to come up with an idea

- meeting someone new

- being stuck in traffic when you're running late

- looking at the mountain of work sitting on your desk

- reading an overly ambitious to-do list

- or even catching a glimpse of that big hairy spider running across the floor

When this happens, the Amygdala instantly places us in "survival mode." It does this by slowing down or shutting off all of the functions it deems non-essential. I'm talking about those silly little time wasters, such as conscious rational thinking, digestion, sexual desire and the ability to access our creative resources. It does this to ensure that we don't waste valuable time and instead places our focus on our instincts. The deeper the Amygdala is triggered, the greater the reaction we experience, and because of this, the less able we are to think and act clearly.

In a sense you could say that we have become *close minded*, not because we're choosing to be stubborn in this case, but as a result of this reactionary fear-based state closing off our ability to access conscious choice.

Instead of acting in a creative way, when the Amygdala is triggered, we react based on past memory of similar threats and instinctive subconscious programming. This isn't necessarily a bad thing. It can certainly come in handy when our survival is *really* at stake, such as it would be if a car were barreling toward us, head on, in our own lane on the highway!

When we are in danger and time is of the essence, we need to react without analyzing. In this case we would need to swerve at just the right time, to change lanes or to react in whatever way was necessary to ensure our safety.

Thankfully, the subconscious mind has a knack for taking care of such reactions. Perhaps you've experienced an automatic reaction that got you out of a situation in just the nick of time. You can thank the Amygdala for that one. Of course, you can imagine that the degree to which we are affected by this fear-based reactionary state directly depends upon the situation we're in. At least it does in most cases. Unfortunately, however, there are exceptions and these exceptions are growing yearly.

As life gets busier and more discomfort is created in our lives by this busy-ness, the Amygdala does not always save its survival instincts for extreme moments. More often than not, in this fast-paced age of technology, it is being triggered by the simplest of things, like a red light when we're in a hurry, or the test that we crammed for intensely, but fear that we might not pass. It is even being triggered today by the overwhelm and discomfort we feel from all of the unseen data and energy floating around in the air through all of our technology. The number of those affected by electro magnetic hypersensitivity is growing at an alarming rate. This discomfort of course has an affect on the Amygdala. In turn, all parts of our being are suffering to some degree. As a result of this overload of energy, many people are walking around in a mental fog, unable to think clearly. Why? Because the Amygdala has restricted our access to the conscious thinking, creative parts of our brains.

How about you? Have you ever found yourself too close to power line towers and as a result do you remember feeling a strange, uncomfortable buzz within your body? Energy is not contained within the wires. It spreads out and permeates everything. To a lesser degree, we are all being exposed to this electro magnetic energy on a daily basis... even while we sleep.

With all the stress we encounter on a daily basis, is it any wonder why so many of us find it difficult to experience true happiness and relaxation to any real degree? The truth is, when we are overwhelmed, afraid, uncomfortable or stressed in any way, happiness has little chance of being experienced.

But fear not!

By understanding and acknowledging what is happening with the

Amygdala, we can begin to take steps to put fear in its place. We can stop the Amygdala from running amok in our lives and through the use of simple creative techniques we can begin to disarm the fear and discomfort that has been holding us back. By doing so we can choose to control our sense of inner peace, which naturally opens the door for happiness to be experienced authentically.

To understand the Amygdala, it can be helpful to identify the three main ways that we typically react when it's triggered.

In the presence of discomfort or fear, our instinctual impulses generally lead us to:

1. Fight,
2. Take flight, or
3. Freeze

When we **fight**, we are reacting aggressively, on both a physical and emotional level, based on our impulsive response to the situation. This is done through physical or verbal means. In effect we are fighting back in response to the strong negative emotional charge we are feeling. The stronger the emotion, the fiercer we fight.

It is not always necessary for another person to be present and involved in these moments. We may often find ourselves impulsively engaging in self-destructive habits as a means of fighting off the way that we are feeling. The war we wage in these moments is internal. It is between us and ourselves and often results in the use of negative self talk, or self inflicted physical abuse, such as cutting and eating disorders, along with drugs, alcohol, sexual addictions, or any number of various *weapons of choice* that we feel will help us to temporarily *beat* our situation and negative feelings. Our actions in these tense moments are rebellious, often spiteful, and reactive in a defiant, aggressive, self destructive way.

When we take **flight**, we find ourselves withdrawing physically and/or emotionally in an attempt to flee the situation. This fleeing can occur through social, physical, or emotional withdrawal. Fleeing can also account for many of the various addictions we have. We *run away* from our problems or fears in an attempt to cover-up or escape from the way we are feeling.

When we **freeze**, we find ourselves shutting down in order to become invisible or inconspicuous. We do this as a way to hide from our situation or feelings. Like a deer in the headlights, we simply cannot think or see clearly and so we stay where we are, stuck in one place. Decisions are difficult to make in this state of fear-based mind fog, and so we don't make them. The actions we need to take are also not clear or easy, and so we don't take any action at all. Procrastination is a prime example of freezing.

By understanding what is happening to us when we find ourselves reacting in the ways mentioned above, we can then take steps to change our experience. The good news is, this awareness alone is actually the first and most important step on the path to authentic change. As we pay attention to how we are feeling, without judgment, we create an opportunity to choose our actions. A spark is created. Change is made. We can choose to relax and disarm the Amygdala. The *really* good news is, even the slightest degree of relaxation will naturally result in an increase of happiness, inner peace, and true success.

One of the simplest methods to begin the process of relaxation is by choosing to breathe slowly and deeply in a conscious way.

Each tiny step that we take toward relaxation begins to create gentle momentum that will grow into even greater levels of relaxation and happiness. And the best part is that we can experience this on a daily basis through Kaizen small steps and everyday creativity.

Even though, at times, we might want to take giant leaps in order to experience the greatest amount of change possible, it is wise to keep our steps small -- at least at first. This might sound strange, but the truth is that even too much relaxation, when we're not used to it, creates the possibility of moving us out of our expected "comfort zone" of discomfort, and as a result, the Amygdala is triggered once again.

Now, you might be saying to yourself, "Oh to be free of the Amygdala! Imagine what we could accomplish without the presence of fear."

I've said this myself in the past, and I've heard many of my clients and students say it too. However, if we take just a moment to consider the situation more carefully, it's easy to see that fear in itself is not the problem. In fact, fear is fairly harmless in and of itself. In fact there are moments when fear can actually be quite invigorating. No, it's not fear that's the real problem, it's our *reaction* to fear and the *resistance* that we create in order to *avoid* fear that is the real problem for everybody! This resistance, tension, and stress is what closes us off from the experience of true happiness, not the fear itself. By accepting that fear is a natural part of life, we can choose to meet it head on in a way that allows us to let go and relax a little bit more each day. By understanding that particular experiences in our lives will trigger the Amygdala, we can take steps to work *with* this process, rather than struggling against it. Through conscious creative choice we can

49

allow fear to be transformed into a level of excitement that has the potential to propel us forward toward our dreams.

The benefits of relaxation:

By coming to peace with where we are in our lives, without resistance, worry, or stress, we open a channel within ourselves that allows success and happiness to flow through us freely. Some of the many benefits we can experience by relaxing are the following:

- Expanded awareness
- Increased mental clarity and focus
- Greater emotional balance
- Improved energy and vitality
- General health improvements in all ways
- Increased access to creative resources
- Discovery of hidden talents and other abilities
- Life becomes easier and more enjoyable
- Negative, unhealthy habits begin to drop away
- We experience greater happiness, true success, and inner peace in all parts of life

Life is meant to be a joy. It is meant to be lived happily and fully. This does not, however, mean that it is meant to be lived completely free from challenges, discomfort or fear. Without the challenges that are present in our lives, we could never grow to our full potential. We could never learn some of the greatest lessons in life about love, compassion, resilience and creativity. What a terrible loss that would be!

Thankfully, in the right frame of mind, our challenges need not be cause for excessive grief. Remember, life is always working in our favor, whether this appears to be the case or not. Even the most difficult challenges are provided *for* us. They help us to grow and to live wholeheartedly. In this sense they can be seen as stepping-stones that lead to something greater. By learning how to relax, this process becomes far easier.

How do you allow yourself to relax?

In the following creative exploration section, we will be taking a look at a few of the various methods that you might like to try in order to increase your experience of relaxation on a daily basis. Remember, the more that you *use* these techniques in a hands-on way, the greater your experience will be. Happiness cannot be talked about or experienced by simply reading a book, not even this book. It needs to be set free through creative techniques!

Creative Exploration

Creativity is a surefire way to increase your ability to relax and experience happiness. But as you will recall, when the Amygdala is triggered, we lose our ability to access our creative resources.

Sounds a bit like the riddle...

"Which came first, the chicken or the egg?"

Thankfully, there is a simple answer this seemingly impossible question. The trick is... you just need to change the way that you look at creativity!

We'll be taking a closer look at what true creativity means in a few chapters from now, but for the time being, how about we focus on CREATING a relaxing, conscious breath to start?

Are you ready to relax and tap into your own creativity?

1. CONSCIOUS "CREATIVE" BREATHING:

Inhale slowly through the nose: As you breathe in life-giving energy, ask yourself, what would you like to feel?

- Relaxation
- Creativity
- Resilience
- Awareness
- Focus
- Clarity
- Happiness
- Authentic Success
- Inner Peace
- Or_____ name your feeling

As you pay attention to the breath and the feeling you would like to experience, notice how the energy begins to take on particular qualities that reflect the feeling you are eliciting. You can do this in the following way:

See this energy flowing into your body with the breath. Imagine the color of the energy, the density, the movement and any other visual qualities that may be present as you breathe in.

Note: If you find it challenging to imagine the various qualities of this energy, ask yourself what it might look like if you could see this energy. This can be a great first step in this creative process. You can do the same for all of the senses. You can also help the experience to grow far more deeply by remembering a time in the past when you experienced one of the feelings you would like to elicit. Memories based on feeling and emotion are powerful. They can be used both positively and negatively; the choice is yours as to which way you experience them.

Hear the energy as it flows into your body with the breath. Notice the tone, the volume, the tempo and any other qualities that may be present.

Feel the energy as it flows into your body with the breath. Notice the texture, the sensation, and the area of your body that is attracting the most energy.

Exhale slowly: You might like to imagine that you are blowing bubbles like a kid with a bubble wand. Go ahead, dip the wand into the bubble soap, lift it up slowly and blow gently. As you release the breath through a small space between your lips, imagine the bubbles forming one by one and floating away. Within each bubble notice all of your cares and concerns being lifted from you and floating away. Notice all of the tension that may be present in your body being released with each bubble. See it floating away into the distance, allowing you to feel relaxed and at peace. Feel free to continue this process for as long as you like; one breath, two, or three, perhaps for a few minutes, or more. I do, however, suggest limiting your time to no more than 20 minutes of conscious creative breathing.

2. CREATE A SENSATIONAL EXPERIENCE:

Take a moment at some point in the day to pay attention to your surroundings. Watch, listen and sense the qualities of the sights, sounds and feelings very carefully. See the way that the light plays on the objects that surround you. Notice the qualities of the sounds as well as the scent in the air. Taste what you are eating if you do this exercise during a meal. Feel the textures of things that are near you. Notice the details through all of your senses and if possible write a quick note about your experience.

Bringing your attention directly to the moment of now can help you to relax immensely. You can do this in a natural, creative way by tapping into your outer senses, and paying attention to what you are experiencing in the current moment physically. In this way you cannot be focusing on the fear of the future or regretting the past. You are just too busy living your life in the here and now today.

By noticing the qualities of the current moment through your senses, you also create an opportunity to realize that you are, in fact ok, no matter what is happening outwardly. Even if your current situation is challenging, you are still here, you are still able to breathe, and to function in some way. You are alive in the moment. This simple shift in awareness, in most cases, creates the opportunity for you to experience a greater sense of focused presence in your world, which naturally results in an increased level of relaxation.

In this exercise, once again, you are focusing on what you are seeing, hearing, and feeling or sensing in all ways. You are paying attention to the qualities of the sights, sounds and feelings, but you are doing so with your eyes and ears wide open rather than using your imagination. You are using your powers of observation, and by doing so you are also increasing your level of mindful awareness, which has the power to relax you even more deeply.

3. YOUR CREATIVE ESCAPE

With or without a visual prompt, allow yourself to enter into a daydream. Imagine a secret world within yourself that reflects your inner state of being. It might be easier to begin this process with a prompt, such as a photo of a beautiful place, be it in nature or anywhere that allows you to feel a sense of peace and ease. You might see yourself in any of the following areas or scenarios:

- Garden
- Mansion
- Beach
- Mountain path or retreat
- On a boat, drifting on a peaceful lake
- Soaring like a bird in the sky
- Floating in space among the stars
- Sitting in front of a glowing fire
- Swimming in the deep like a dolphin
- Or _____ name your place

Allow yourself to create ideal conditions within your daydream. This is YOUR world. You get to create the conditions that are exactly right for you, in whatever way you want to.

Choosing to experience surroundings that elicit feelings of happiness, peace, beauty, harmony, abundance and all good things here in your daydream can have a profound effect on you in many wonderful ways. The more that you immerse yourself in the experience, the more positive effects that you will begin to experience physically as well as emotionally and mentally.

Once again, you can do this for as little as a few seconds and as long as 20 to 30 minutes.

Simplicity is the essence of happiness

Unknown

E... ESSENCE

Isn't happiness what we've been

dreaming about all along?

Kaizenized Quick Notes

- *Our physical goals, dreams and desires for material gain or personal experiences are merely symbols of a deeper longing to experience a particular feeling. This feeling can often be described as the essence of happiness in its many forms.*

- *Until we can allow ourselves to let go of the attachment we have to our external symbols of happiness and allow ourselves instead to tap into the presence of this essence or feeling that is always present within, we will constantly be chasing our bliss like a carrot suspended in front of a horse; with each step that we take, what we believe to be happiness also moves a step away.*

- *By understanding what the **essence** of happiness means to us in a personal way, we increase our chances of truly feeling it. Without understanding what this essence means to us as individuals, how can we ever really know when we've achieved it? How long will we continue to search for happiness in all the wrong places?*

- *By recalling what the energy of happiness feels like, sounds like, looks like, tastes like and smells like, we can draw to mind our memories of being filled with this energy. By doing so we are then able to elicit the essential qualities of the experience of happiness in any given moment. We do by simply remembering where happiness exists within us and allowing ourselves to tap into it once again.*

- *Happiness never truly goes away (just as electricity doesn't disappear when we turn off a light switch).*
  However, the channel to happiness does close from time to time when we are stressed, and resistant in some way. By focusing on the essence of happiness, however, through the use of simple creative techniques, we can easily flip the switch, turn off the Amygdala and reopen the channel to happiness whenever we choose to. Yes, this can be just as easy as turning on the lights in our home.

The Extended Version

What are we really searching for?

We're searching for money, toys, vacations, a fabulous body, a beautiful face, a new boyfriend, girlfriend, husband, wife, a baby, a great job, flattering clothes, a fancy car, the newest phone, the latest gadget or other form of technology. Year after year we continue to seek all of the *things* that we "think" will bring more joy, fun, and satisfaction *into* our lives. These are all wonderful goals that we can work toward and acquire, but they are just that: "goals." Once achieved, these goals simply lead to even more and more goals in this never ending cycle of desire and acquisition that we mistakenly call the pursuit of happiness.

It makes me crazy just thinking about it. If we continue to base our happiness on the attainment of these goals, how will we ever be able to experience true inner peace? These things don't bring us happiness. What they do bring us is a sense of DESIRE, which leads to ATTACHMENT to a goal, a person, an experience or a thing. Then, once our goal or desire is attained, what happens next? ANTICLIMAX hits hard like the crash we experience after a sugar rush. What follows this? More goals, more desires, and more crashes! Wouldn't you agree that this sounds a little bit, or rather a LOT, like addiction? It certainly does to me.

This is not HAPPINESS. This, in fact, is addiction to desires, plain and simple. And sadly, we are *all* susceptible to this addictive cycle. But thankfully there is an easy solution to this dilemma that if implemented through the use of Kaizen small steps, can actually be quite enjoyable.

Before I share more about these Kaizen small steps, though, I'd like to clarify one thing. I'm not saying we should never *want* anything or create goals for ourselves. What fun would life be without any desire, without anything to look forward to or strive for? Why would we bother to get up in the morning if there were no goals to work toward, or dreams to create? No, I'm *definitely* not suggesting that we give up on our dreams. What I am suggesting is that we let go of the intense, white knuckle *death grip,* unhealthy level of *attachment* to the *way* that our dreams and desires unfold and are ultimately fulfilled. It's the attachment to the *details* that's the real happiness killer here, not the overall dream or desire. So how can we create some balance here? What might the solution be? Depending on your situation, there can be many.

I have found that by simply looking a little deeper into what we want, and why we want it, along with our timeframe of when we want to receive it and how we believe that we will FEEL when we have it, we naturally begin to relax our attachment to the details of *it*. Through this deeper exploration we are able to experience the positive results of conscious awareness, as opposed to negative effects of impulse and attachment. In turn this state of increased awareness and relaxation opens up greater potential within us while it provides new opportunities that we never dreamed possible while we were so focused on the way that we *thought* things *should* be! Sounds like a win-win situation, doesn't it? If you agree, and if you are willing to try this new approach to creating your dreams, the first question I have for you is this:

What do you *REALLY* want?

Considering you're here, right now, reading this book, I think it's fair to say that your goal or desire is happiness, which of course is great! But how will you know when you've achieved this wonderful goal? How will you *feel* when happiness comes knocking on the door of your heart? Please don't just say, *"Well, happy, of course!"* Because the truth is, the *word* happiness means very little. Then again, it can also mean *many* things. The question is...

What does true happiness mean to you?

In order to answer this question to any degree beyond the superficial level, we will have to dig deeper. Here's an example of what I mean...

Let's look at Georgette, who dreams of one day owning a Corvette. This girl has had her heart set on getting her hands on one of these cars for longer than she can remember. In her heart and in her mind she truly thinks that owning a Corvette will make her HAPPY.

But let me ask you, what do you think is really going on here?

What does Georgette really want?

What is the *feeling* she is looking to find?

What will owning a Corvette do for her... really?

Georgette's answer to this question was: freedom, exhilaration, power, and the sense of being truly alive. When asked again what *those* feelings all boiled down to, Georgette's response was **HAPPINESS,** of course!

So, in essence, Georgette is not *really* looking for a Corvette per se. *(Even though it is a super cool car to own.)* She is actually looking for HAPPINESS! The Corvette, she believes, will provide her with this happiness. But really, when it comes right down to it, the car is merely a symbol for this essential feeling that she wishes to achieve... the feeling that is already inside of her just waiting to be released.

Fast forward to a few months into the future. Let's say that Georgette was successful. She bought the car of her dreams and has been driving it for about a month now. At first she had a great time: top down, wind blasting through her hair, pedal to the metal baby, hugging the corners, feeling the adrenaline rush, loving the speed, enjoying the responsive handling of this beautiful machine and embracing the freedom to GO! But then come the flashing lights followed by the ticket, the fine and the points on her driver's license.

Ugh! Not fun and certainly not happy.

Next come the payments for not only the ticket but also for the car loan. Of course all of this happened right on the very same day that her refrigerator broke down. Then as if that wasn't bad enough, there, sitting on her desk, was a pink slip waiting for her when she arrived at work. Ouch! Bad day... Cue dramatic music. Georgette hangs her head, looks at the car in sorrowful frustration and kicks the tire, not once but repetitively. She now blames the car for her unhappiness.

Of course, this is one BIG anti-climax and thankfully not all experiences will be quite as dramatic, but I'm guessing that you're getting the picture here.

Georgette got what she'd always wanted: She acquired the car of her dreams. In fact, it's sitting in her garage, but now when she drives it, she is not feeling as happy as she thought she would. What she *is* feeling is stress. In fact, at the moment she actually regrets buying the car. So what does she do now?

There are many things that Georgette could do, but one of the most helpful things at this point would be to relax, to let go of her fear and explore the possibilities that are available to her with an open mind, unaffected by the Amygdala. At the same time it might be helpful for her to explore what true happiness *actually* means to her in a much deeper sense... *essentially*.

Georgette has learned that the car was just a symbol for happiness in her life. Now she has an opportunity to discover what happiness truly means to her, in a deeper and more authentic way. In this sense her experience could actually be viewed as a blessing. Of course Georgette is not seeing it this way... yet.

A rose by any other name would smell as sweet

Every word in every language is simply a symbol for a particular sight, sound, feeling, taste, smell, type of knowledge, or a combination of these things. We apply words or terms to things and experiences, in the hopes that we will collectively understand each other. To a certain point this method works quite nicely. But in other circumstances, words can certainly fail us miserably because each of us as an individual applies a deeper meaning to our words based on our personal memories and preferences, along with our life circumstances. Therefore, in order to *truly* understand each other and be understood in return, it can be helpful to dig deeper, into the essence of a word, rather than relying on its superficial meaning. By doing so we will experience ourselves communicating in a far more effective way with the world around us. We may also find during the process that we are better able to understand our own thoughts and feelings as well.

Do you recall, earlier in the book, how I mentioned a client of mine who would not allow herself to want happiness. She avoided using this particular word as it brought up fear in her. She was afraid that she would experience disappointed if she was not successful in achieving true happiness.

Remember how adamant she was about the fact that she simply wanted contentment and the feeling of being safe? As we discovered, to her, this was happiness in **essence**.

Now I'd like to ask you what you think. What words describe happiness to you? Please take a moment to check off as many words below that symbolize true happiness in your heart and mind.

There are no right or wrong answers, so please do not overthink this exercise. Just quickly fly through and feel the energy of the words as you read them.

Notice which ones resonate with you. Tick them off when they do.

- ☐ Abundance
- ☐ Appreciation
- ☐ Blessedness
- ☐ Bliss
- ☐ Cheerfulness
- ☐ Contentment
- ☐ Delight
- ☐ Delirium
- ☐ Ecstasy
- ☐ Elation
- ☐ Enchantment
- ☐ Enjoyment
- ☐ Euphoria
- ☐ Exhilaration
- ☐ Exuberance
- ☐ Giddy
- ☐ Gladness
- ☐ Glee
- ☐ Glory
- ☐ Good health
- ☐ Good humor
- ☐ Good spirits
- ☐ Gratitude

- ☐ Hopefulness
- ☐ Inner peace
- ☐ Jolly
- ☐ Joy
- ☐ Jubilation
- ☐ Lighthearted
- ☐ Love
- ☐ Merriment
- ☐ Mindful
- ☐ Optimism
- ☐ Peace of mind
- ☐ Playfulness
- ☐ Pleasure
- ☐ Prosperity
- ☐ Safety
- ☐ Satisfaction
- ☐ Thankfulness
- ☐ Warm-hearted
- ☐ Well-being
- ☐ Whole hearted
- ☐ Youthfulness
- ☐ Zest for life
- ☐ Zippity-doo-dah

How did it feel for you to go through the list and see all of these expressions for the essence of happiness? This list by no means is complete, but it does give you a little taste of how much more there is to the overall picture of happiness.

In order to create a well rounded experience, I'd also like to ask you to make note of any words on this list that you felt did not accurately describe true happiness to you.

I'd also like to ask if there were any *other* words that popped into your mind which were not on the list? How did it make you feel to sense their absence?

Did you experience yourself judging this experience along with each individual word? Did you find yourself weighing the significance of each word in the grand scheme of what HAPPINESS truly means?

If so, once again, I have to say you're not alone. But in the same breath I really must add...

What a waste of time and energy!

Why bother judging the meaning of a symbol when you can...

Just be happy!

By judging, our minds begin to close down. Our hearts quickly follow suit. At times this happens just a little bit, while other times it happens a lot. Every time our hearts close down a certain degree of tension (disguised as judgment) sets in, and before we know it...

BAM, *there goes that skittish Amygdala once again!*

And there goes happiness right along with it, locked up tight behind the doors of a closed mind. This, of course is due to the resistance and fear that is experienced as a result of triggering the Amygdala and the limited access to the very resources we want and need in the process.

As mentioned earlier, it can often be helpful and necessary to acknowledge what "*is not*" in order to understand "*what is.*" The same can be said about acknowledging what is *unhelpful* in order to discover the truth of what will *help* us to *create* a greater experience of happiness. Hopefully at this point, through the exercise above, you can see that judgment will *never* help you to experience more happiness. Discernment and conscious choice, on the other hand, however, will.

Now, at this point, we know that things in and of themselves can't make us happy and judgment certainly won't make us happy either, so what *will*? What actually has the power to bring this essential feeling to life within us in an experiential way? What is the trick, you might ask? I too asked that question many times. The answer I found is very simply...

JUST ENJOY HAPPINESS FOR WHAT IT IS!

By letting go of labels, and replacing them with experiences, we can use our energy wisely in a way that helps us to enjoy life to a far greater degree while allowing for even happier experiences to be. Without the resistance of judgment, we leave the door to the heart and mind wide open, allowing room for happy miracles to come through for us at just the right time, and in just the right way. When we start judging, however, that door begins to close again. But thankfully it doesn't have to, if we

68

choose not to engage in labeling.

Stop right there!

Let go of that impulse to judge based on the way that you *think* things *should* be and **JUST BE HAPPY** for goodness sake, even if it's just for a few seconds at a time.   You'll be glad you did.

Eliciting the essence of true happiness, the easy way

How did that last paragraph make you feel? When you read the words JUST BE HAPPY, did it take a load off? Or did it tick you off?   Did you say to yourself, *"If only it was that easy!"* Well, the truth is, it *can* be this easy when you know how to elicit the essence and energy of true happiness from deep within yourself where it exists naturally.

In fact, its as easy as 1... 2... 3!

Let's take a look to see what I mean:

1.   The first step is simply **REMEMBERING** what it FEELS like to BE HAPPY by tapping into the happiness memories stored in your subconscious programming.

Do you remember what happiness feels like experientially? If not, can you imagine what it would feel like right now to be happy? Take a moment to close your eyes and remember a time when you were happy and how that felt to you, or imagine what it might feel like to be happy right now. Then go ahead and jot down a quick note in your journal about this. List any feelings that come to mind which can help to make this step feel more complete. Does it feel warm, loving, light and free, bubbling over... happy.

69

How else does it feel?

2. Step two: If this is tricky for you to do, I suggest that you allow yourself to **RELAX** and get comfortable where you are. Take a few deep, slow breaths, then think again, very gently now. Continuing to breathe deeply and consciously as you do, deeper and even deeper still, relaxing more and more, bit by bit, step by gentle step, allow yourself to tap into those happy memories or your happy imaginings that may be hiding deep within you. When you're relaxed and feeling ready, go ahead and explore the following:

- Can you recall a moment in your life when you felt a shift take place within you, like the parting of the clouds on a dark and stormy day?
- If not... can you imagine what that *might* feel like?
- Can you remember feeling a wave of warm love wash through you like the sun's rays that burst through the clouds in shafts of light, and regardless of what was or was not happening at the moment, everything just felt right in your world?
- If not, can you imagine what this *might* feel like?
- Do you remember feeling safe and loved and exactly where you were meant to be, even for a short moment in time? Do you remember being aware of the fact that somewhere inside of yourself you just *knew* that everything was going to be ok?
- If you cannot remember a specific moment like this, can you instead imagine what that *might* be like?

Does any of this sound familiar?

Do you remember feeling this way?

If not, are you able to imagine what this might have felt like and in doing so are you able to feel it now, instinctively?

I can understand that you might be saying to yourself at this point, *"Oh for goodness' sake, Pam. Why not just tell me what happiness is, and what it feels like, so that we can get on with it already? Isn't this what books normally do?"*

True enough. Books do typically express the opinion, knowledge and the experience of the writer, and of course this book does, too. But at the same time, this particular book is a little different. In fact, my hope is that it is a LOT different for you.

If you would have found the secret to eliciting true happiness already, by listening to other people, or reading the words that they wrote, you certainly would not be here today with this book in your hand… would you?

Unlike other books you've read in the past, this one is not *only* meant to be a source of information and resources in the form of tools and techniques. Much more than that, it is my intention, as your guide, to provide you with a catalyst that can help YOU to **open your own mind in a way that reveals the truth about happiness that is already present inside of you**. In this case I'm not actually writing this book in an effort to *teach* you anything. Rather, I'm writing to help you **remember what you already know**. I'm providing you with a creative way to enter

71

into the depths of your authentic state of being; your creative self, that lies on the other side of your subconscious programs, where true happiness, authentic success and the eternal state of inner peace already exists.

3. Step three: As you describe the sensations present in the feeling of happiness, notice how you, on some level, are actually **EXPERIENCING** it again! How 'bout that? Now, this is only the beginning of something much greater, but it is a powerful beginning nevertheless. If you even sense a micro mini bit of a feeling, you have made progress!
   Just like planting a seed, and providing the conditions that allow it to germinate *(in this case, practicing this technique in small increments of time, numerous times per week)*, you can allow this feeling to grow into something much greater. Just as the towering oak was once a little acorn, filled with the essence of the full grown tree, so too is the essence, energy and potential of true happiness waiting to grow inside of you!

Through the use of this exercise and the three step process in which you allow yourself to...

1. REMEMBER
2. RELAX
3. EXPERIENCE

...we can realize that everything we wish to feel, along with all of the resources we feel that we need, are already present within us. There is nothing that is outside of us, ever. By acknowledging this fact, we consciously take back our power to elicit happiness from within. In doing so, we allow ourselves to break free from the seductive lure of goal addiction, constant desire and attachment to superficial details. In essence we begin to live as we were always meant to live, as happy, abundant, consciously creative BEings.

As you move through this book, one chapter, sentence, or word at a time, you will begin to see how important this particular level of awareness is, and how you can combine this awareness with certain techniques in order to *choose* to *create* authentic happiness in any given moment, in any given time, no matter what is happening in your life externally.

Creative Exploration

The energy of authentic happiness, true success and inner peace is experienced through the senses, both outwardly in the form of physical experience, and also inwardly in the form of memory, imagination and intuition.

The following exercises can help you to bring yourself into greater alignment with happy energy, while at the same time helping you to raise your level of awareness as to *how* you are experiencing this energy on a *daily basis*.

1. Under The Microscope
Allow yourself to relax a little with a calming breath or two. Then begin to recall the qualities of energy that you experienced in our last chapter's conscious creative breathing exercise: *relaxation, creativity, resilience, awareness, focus, clarity,*

happiness, authentic, success, inner peace, or something else you wanted to feel in your relaxing breath.

In this particular exercise we will be taking a closer look at this quality of energy, exploring it in a much deeper way. When you're ready, allow yourself to get as comfortable as possible, and let's begin.

Imagine for a moment that you have a powerful microscope in front of you. Through the use of your creative imagination, place a little of your "happy energy" on a slide that you place under the microscope.

As you turn the dials and focus in, imagine that you can see an image beginning to unfold. It might first appear to look like a group of cells with a membrane and nucleus, but watch as the image transforms each time you dial in closer. Little by little each cell begins to take shape. Together they become part of a scene, like a community of cells personified in some special way. Watch as each cell moves about, engaged in happy activity. Notice how peaceful each one is in its own unique way. Notice how this makes you feel.

In my own experience with this exercise, I saw the image of my happy energy coming through in the form of the characters from Dr. Seuss' book **Horton Hears a Who***. Each little happy Who in my own happy Whoville was singing and dancing. They were exploring their world through playful activity. The sun was shining, its light reflected on the ripples of the lake like tiny sparkling diamonds. It was a warm and peaceful day. Everyone enjoyed his or her place in the community. There was a place for everybody. Happiness flowed freely in this experience. It existed everywhere* *the eye could see.*

How about you? What do *you* see in your own microscope?

Be gentle with yourself as you do this exercise. Creativity and relaxation can never be forced, but rather, they must be allowed to flow through. This being the case, if it is difficult for you to imagine your scene, ask yourself what you *might* see if the image was a little clearer. Also note that often people do not "see" in the form of pictures on an inner screen of the mind, but rather they "sense" the presence of an image. Either way, the scene that comes through for you is perfectly fine. There is no need to judge what you are experiencing, just notice what you can and let it be what it is authentically. Then pay attention to how this experience makes you feel. Jot down a quick note about any sights and feelings you may be experiencing in any way, along with how you believe these sights may be showing you ways to bring more happiness into your "real" life.

For me this meant adding a little more playfulness into my life. It meant letting go of some of my seriousness and allowing myself to fully explore my environment in a lighthearted, curious way. It meant connecting with nature on a regular basis and adding music to my days.   By the way, this exercise has worked beautifully for me and it can work for you too if you let it.

2. Turn Up The Volume; Tune In To The Frequency

Continuing with the experience above, I invite you now to add an awareness of sound to the scenario that's playing out.

Imagine that you have some high powered speakers connected to your microscope. These speakers can detect and transmit the sound of energy. Take note of the sounds that you might be hearing, or sensing in any way. Again, hearing can also present itself inwardly in the form of intuition. These sounds can also come through in the form of self talk or inner narrations, similar to listening to someone tell you a story.

How are you perceiving the sounds in your experience? What messages do you feel these particular sounds are sharing with you regarding the circumstances of your outer life?

How could you use this information to bring a greater experience of happiness into your days? How does this make you feel?

3.   Where In Your Body Has Happiness Been Hiding?

Most people automatically assume that happiness exists mainly in their heart, while others believe its presence is felt predominantly in their head. Occasionally some people sense happiness in the core of their being, like a "gut feeling." But the truth is, authentic happiness exists within *every* cell in the body... right down to your baby toes!

Take a moment now to zone in on a particular part of your body. For example, you might choose to focus on your feet.

Now, imagine all of the cells in your feet smiling with joy. Feel the energy of happiness flowing through the blood that courses through the veins. Notice the sensation of laughter, music, inner peace and other sensations and qualities of happy energy which may be present in the bones and cartilage of your feet as well.

Feel this happiness beginning to grow, expanding, and shining brighter, feeling richer and deeper while it rises up higher and comes to life in your ankles as well as your feet. Notice the presence of increased joyful awareness as it continues to rise up your legs. Feel the happy energy coming to life in your skin now and in all of the major organs in your body. Notice how good it can feel to sense your liver smiling and as it does you know instinctively that because of this happy energy, your liver and other organs are better able to do their jobs with greater efficiency. See how amazing, how powerful and how healing the energy of happiness is! Continue to enjoy this process as you sense the energy of happiness within all parts of your body now.

Again, if you need to, allow yourself to imagine what this might feel like, especially if you are finding this exercise tricky. If you practice this technique on a regular basis I guarantee that in a very short period of time you will be feeling, seeing, hearing and sensing some amazing things in ways that will prove to be wonderfully enriching, life enhancing and creatively empowering.

As you continue with this exercise, you may also notice any areas of your body where it is difficult to feel happiness. Notice any places within yourself that feel numb or disconnected in any way. Perhaps this area is trying to get your attention. It might be telling you that it needs a little more loving care in some way. What message do you feel that this part of your body has for you? Quickly write down any thoughts that come to mind, without questioning yourself or overthinking.

The wisdom of your body is amazing. There is much it can share with you, but only if you listen.

The major value in life is not in what you get, but in what you become.

Unknown

$\mathcal{V}$...   VALUES

"I'd far rather be happy than right any day."

-- Douglas Adams

Kaizenized Quick Notes

- *Certain values, such as love, kindness, natural beauty and authentic inner strength make it easier for us to naturally tap into our innate creative resources and the experience of true happiness. How well this works for us depends on the beliefs that these values are connected to in our subconscious programming. Beliefs and values that come from the heart result in happiness. While those that come from a sense of duty, based on what we believe is expected of us or what has always been, do not.*

- *Certain values, that many of us believe to be admirable, such as strong willpower, hard work, dedication, self-sacrifice, humility and responsibility, can actually block our ability to access true happiness, success and inner peace. Once again, this depends entirely upon the beliefs that these values are connected with in our unconscious programming. Positive beliefs attached to admirable values equals the experience of true happiness, while negative beliefs connected with the same values can be damaging to the individual in a number of ways.*

- *Many people in this world today are not consciously aware of what they truly value.*

- *By raising our awareness of what we value in this life, we can then consciously explore the memories and beliefs they are connected to.*

- *By letting go of outdated beliefs and limitations, which no longer serve to help us grow, we open our hearts and minds in a way that allows for a greater level of happiness to flow through our lives. In the process, the sense of hope and inner peace are renewed in us as well. We discover that the number of opportunities available, at any given moment in time, multiplies significantly as a result of this increased awareness.*

- *It is important to be completely honest in this process if we are to make any true change.*

The Extended Version

What matters most to you?

In your heart you want happiness but deep down it's possible that you may be carrying around values from the past that place the greatest importance on particular things that make it very difficult to truly experience happiness.

- Hard work and self-sacrifice
- Strong will power
- Placing others' needs above your own

Although admirable, the values mentioned above, among others, can actually hold us back from experiencing true joy, unless they are balanced in a healthy way through conscious choice. This choice must be one that is made from the heart, rather than the mind or from a sense of duty. They must also encourage positive self-growth through both giving *and* receiving, along with action that is balanced with rest, and work that is balanced with play.

When I was four or five years old, I loved to do special things for my mom to make her happy. It would fill my heart with so much joy to draw a picture for her, to brush her hair, or to bring her a flower that I picked from the garden outside. It made my heart even happier when I saw the look of happiness on *her* face. This look instantly made me feel warm all over. It made my heart shine with love and it also made me want to do even *more* things to make her happy. In *her* happiness, I was happy, too. By giving, I definitely received.

Most young children naturally have the desire to give, to please, and to want to bring joy to others. This is especially true of children before they enter into the school system and the social consciousness, before society has a chance to introduce to them the cycle of addictive desire in personal ways. When this happens, more focus is naturally placed on the identification of "I" rather than "we," and happiness begins to dwindle accordingly. As we experience a growing number of wants for ourselves, we begin to forget how good it feels to give, just for the sake of giving. In the absence of giving from the heart, a sense of *duty* takes its place. If, at this point, our giving is not done through personal choice, we feel a demand or an obligation that is placed upon us by external sources. At this point we find children doing less and less to make Mom or Dad happy, and instead there are more demands for me, me, me. At this point giving is often done from a state of resistance, and often grudgingly. Of course, this is not true for everyone, but it is common for many. As I look back, I see this pattern present in myself and I also recognize it in my own kids.

Now, this is not necessarily a bad thing. In fact, it's a natural process of life in this world. Think about it for a moment. If we didn't learn how to care for our own needs and ask for what we want in this life, we'd have one heck of a time getting by. We would place all of the responsibility on others to meet our growing needs. How, I must ask, could this ever result in growth or happiness for anybody?

As I'm sure you can see, a little ego is necessary in this lifetime. However, true as that may be, the questions remain...

- Are we aware that this is happening?

- Are we aware of the reasons *why* we do what we do, *why* we want the things we want and what the motives are behind our giving?

- Do we know what matters most to us in this process?

- Are we giving out of a sense of duty? Or are we giving from the heart just because it feels so good to give and to create conditions that have the potential to make it easier for others to choose to be happy?

Could your beliefs be standing in your way?

Take a moment to read the following list, and as you do I invite you to notice which beliefs you hold personally. Please allow yourself to be completely transparent as you do this. No hiding behind excuses, or whitewashing the truth. Go ahead now and check the boxes, even if you *sense* that you "might" believe it even just a little bit:

- ☐ It's better to give than to receive.
- ☐ Money is the root of all evil.
- ☐ It takes hard work to be successful.
- ☐ It is important to be in control at all times.
- ☐ A "good" person avoids hurting someone else, even at the expense of his or her own happiness.
- ☐ You must earn someone's love.
- ☐ You are not worthy of love, prosperity, abundance or any other good things that life has to offer until you do enough or give enough to be worthy.
- ☐ You are not smart enough, talented enough, creative enough, rich enough, beautiful enough, witty enough, thin enough, or strong enough.
- ☐ Others should love you and treat you in a certain way. If they don't, it means they do not care.
- ☐ Nothing I do is ever good enough.
- ☐ I may be wasting my time if I take a chance and follow my dreams.
- ☐ It is important to get really good at multitasking.
- ☐ Being busy and highly productive makes me worthy of others' respect.

☐ Doing nothing is bad, lazy, and unacceptable.

☐ If we want to be happy, it is necessary to think positive thoughts in each moment.

☐ Feeling pain, sadness, grief and other negative things is bad. It must be avoided at all costs.

Now, I'd like to ask you the following questions:

- Did your reaction to any of these statements surprise you?
- Were you aware of how you felt before you read this list?
- How tempted were you to slide through by answering the "right way" for each point?
- Did you slide through???
- Is there really a "right way" to see any of these points?
- Did you find yourself justifying your beliefs in any way?
- And do you believe this justification to be true without a shadow of doubt?
- Do your answers feel good to you? Do they really?

Is it time for a change?

It is natural to take on beliefs from our families, from society, and from past experiences. It is also natural to hold onto these beliefs even when they no longer play a part in our lives. If one person or experience hurt us, we fear that more people and experiences will hurt us in similar ways and so we avoid placing ourselves into situations that cause us to feel vulnerable. But is this helping us to feel happy? I don't think so! In fact, I know that it's not.

Through my own experiences, I discovered that it wasn't until I chose to face my outdated beliefs, and ask some serious awareness raising questions, that I truly began to experience happiness authentically.

How about you? Are you ready to take a deeper look you're your own beliefs in a way that can open up the doors to far greater happiness in all parts of your life? If so, the following list of questions and suggestions can be helpful in a variety of ways. By exploring your beliefs in an open and honest manner, you will naturally find yourself quickly experiencing:

- Greater self-confidence
- A true passion for life
- The ability to accomplish things you once only dreamed possible, and much more. Believe me!

1. **Take another look at the list of limiting beliefs** on the previous page then **choose the top three that seem to have the greatest effect on you.** Alternatively, if there are other beliefs, not listed here, that come to mind for you that you know are holding you back or affecting you in any negative way, please choose those instead.

2. Next, go ahead and **read your list of three limiting beliefs again**. This time notice how your body feels as you read each one. Do you sense tension rising? Is there a lump in your throat? Do you feel any heaviness in your chest or tightness in your

gut? Which statement makes your shoulders rise up to your ears? Which one causes you to want to flee this exercise or fight the feeling and push it away the most?

The belief that causes you the greatest amount of discomfort is NOT the one you will work with initially.

Did I just hear you say *phew*? If so, I'm glad! One of the beliefs that hold many people back in their quest to create positive life change is thinking that in order to accomplish anything significant we need to take on the BIG things first. However, by focusing on the "BIG" things first, we may actually find that we succeed in accomplishing NOTHING at all. Remember what happens when we move too far out of our comfort zone too quickly? That's right, there goes the Amygdala again! Instead of making small consistent changes in a gentle, relaxed way, we end up spiraling into the state of overwhelm, which either causes us to run away into our old habits and self-sabotaging behavior, or we freeze in fear and find ourselves stuck in procrastination with the greatest intentions in mind that we never act upon in any way.

3.   Looking more closely at your second or third most limiting belief now, you might like to ask yourself the following question:

Where do you think this belief came from?

Remember, beliefs can come from a variety of sources, so go ahead and write as many things down as you would like to. For example, do you remember hearing your parents saying the same words that repeat in your mind on a daily basis?

Did these ideas come from something a sibling used to say to you? Do you remember any movies you watched in the past that may have had a strong effect on you? How about books you've read? When we are deeply connected with a story, we can often take on the beliefs, fears and challenges of the characters and on an unconscious level we may believe them to be our own. Does any of this sound familiar? How about advertising, or the news? One of the ways that the media manages to keep us coming back for more, and the advertising companies make sure we buy what they're selling, is by creating a perceived sense of lack or a need that is based on the fear of not having enough. Is this triggering anything for you now? How else might you have adopted your own personal beliefs? How about memories of past experiences? You've heard the saying, *"Once bitten, twice shy."* Could this possibly apply to your own beliefs?

4. Next, ask yourself: **is there is any measure of truth to my belief?** Some fears are present to help protect us in certain ways, while others are simply based on illusion. By weeding out fact from fiction, you can help yourself to feel and experience a greater sense of confidence and clarity. Just because we're looking at ways to let go of limiting beliefs does not mean we need to throw all caution to the wind and act recklessly without any thought or consideration to our safety and well- being. We have the ability to make choices in this life. Why not choose with the best information at hand?

5. **How do you feel your negative beliefs might be holding you back?** Have you been avoiding things that could possibly create greater joy in your life based on fear or a sense of discomfort in any way?

In retrospect, have you ever heard yourself saying...

"If only I could do it over again. If only I could have been a little braver. If only I had the opportunity to do things differently."

6.   **Is there a small step you could take right here and now to move beyond your fears and limiting beliefs?** When I talk about small steps, this could be as simple as the following:

- Acting *as if* you did not have this limiting belief, even for a few seconds at a time, then imagining what life would be like if this were the case. Imagination is the place where all of the greatest accomplishments began. It is the source of positive change.
- Writing down a list of the benefits you could achieve or would like to achieve *as if* they have already been accomplished.
- Daydreaming about a small step you could take, then making the step even smaller until it is so small and simple that you simply cannot help but succeed.

7.   **Take one of the steps mentioned above.**

8.   **Remember that small steps have the potential to add up quickly.** Each time you allow yourself to look at your beliefs honestly and challenge them in any way, the less hold they have on you in a negative sense. At the same time, the opposite is true for the positive, helpful beliefs you hold within you. By focusing on the goodness in your life along with the wonderful qualities you value, the more you will draw these qualities to you.

Creative Exploration

1. **Core values exercise:**
    - Look at the extensive list of values on the following pages. Begin checking the boxes beside the words that resonate with you. Notice especially the ones that FEEL energetically appealing. Also notice the ones you feel a particular level of resistance to. You might like to highlight these for future reference.
    - Next, go back and fine tune your list by choosing the top 20 of those that you checked off in which you feel most connection.
    - Allow the list to sit for a little while. Then when you feel ready, go back and choose your top 10 out of the 20. At this point you will want to pay close attention to how these choices FEEL energetically within your body.
    - Now its time to fine-tune your choices and select your top 5 values. Pay even closer attention to what these choices LOOK like, FEEL like and SOUND like within you, energetically. Notice which values that you are drawn to AUTHENTICALLY, rather than those that you *think* you *should* choose.

You also might like to pay attention to the STORIES that these words bring up within you.

    - Each time you choose and re-choose your values, fine tuning your awareness more and more clearly, I invite you to pay close attention to where you are feeling a predominate sense of energy within your body.

Do you feel the greatest energy in your:

FOREHEAD	*STOMACH*	*LEGS*
THROAT	*SOLAR PLEXUS*	*HANDS*
CHEST	*PELVIS*	*FEET*
HEART	*BACK*	*OR ?*

Go ahead and take quick notes of what you are feeling as you do this exercise, then notice how these notes are making you feel. Ask yourself, what this feeling reminds you of? Journaling about this feeling can be an enlightening experience. To take the process even further, you might want to ask the energy itself what message it would like to share with you. You may wish to allow the energy to write a letter *to you* through your hand in which it conveys a message to you ABOUT you.

- Notice how this entire process feels to you. What does it bring up within you? What does it remind you of?

- Take your time as you move through this experience. There is no rush.

- You may continue to explore this week by week as you continue to read this book.

- Once you have shortened your list to five choices, put the list away for three days.

During this time notice anything that "shines" or stands out to you predominantly in your daily life, as your mind will continue to chew on the process.

- As such, pay particular attention to your dreams. What symbolism is present?
- Notice any inner nudges or sensations. What is being released by your subconscious?
- Notice any synchronicities or other "odd" occurrences. How is the process changing things in your life for you.
- After three days take out your list again and re-read it. Check back in with your body. Is your list still true, or has a greater truth come through in the process?

Whether or not you have explored your core values in the past, I encourage you to do this exercise again through new eyes and with an open mind and heart. By embarking upon this process with a sense of curiosity, you might be amazed at what you can discover in yourself.

"Would you tell me, please, which way I ought to go from here?"

"That depends a good deal on where you want to get to," said the Cat.

"I don't much care where," said Alice.

"Then it doesn't matter which way you go," said the Cat.

Alice in Wonderland

CORE VALUES LIST:

- ☐ Acceptance
- ☐ Accessibility
- ☐ Accomplishment
- ☐ Accountability
- ☐ Accuracy
- ☐ Achievement
- ☐ Acknowledgement
- ☐ Activeness
- ☐ Adaptability
- ☐ Adoration
- ☐ Advancement
- ☐ Adventure
- ☐ Affection
- ☐ Agility
- ☐ Alertness
- ☐ Altruism
- ☐ Amazement
- ☐ Ambition
- ☐ Amusement
- ☐ Anticipation
- ☐ Appreciation
- ☐ Approachability
- ☐ Approval
- ☐ Art
- ☐ Articulacy
- ☐ Artistry
- ☐ Assertiveness
- ☐ Attentiveness
- ☐ Attractiveness
- ☐ Audacity
- ☐ Availability
- ☐ Awareness
- ☐ Awe
- ☐ Balance
- ☐ Beauty
- ☐ Being the best
- ☐ Belonging
- ☐ Benevolence
- ☐ Bliss
- ☐ Boldness
- ☐ Bravery
- ☐ Brilliance
- ☐ Calmness
- ☐ Capability
- ☐ Care
- ☐ Carefulness
- ☐ Celebrity
- ☐ Certainty
- ☐ Challenge
- ☐ Change
- ☐ Charity
- ☐ Cheerfulness
- ☐ Clarity
- ☐ Cleanliness
- ☐ Cleverness
- ☐ Closeness
- ☐ Comfort
- ☐ Commitment
- ☐ Community

- ☐ Compassion
- ☐ Competence
- ☐ Competition
- ☐ Completion
- ☐ Composure
- ☐ Concentration
- ☐ Confidence
- ☐ Conformity
- ☐ Congruency
- ☐ Connection
- ☐ Consciousness
- ☐ Consistency
- ☐ Contentment
- ☐ Continuity
- ☐ Contribution
- ☐ Control
- ☐ Conviction
- ☐ Coolness
- ☐ Cooperation
- ☐ Cordiality
- ☐ Correctness
- ☐ Country
- ☐ Courage
- ☐ Courtesy
- ☐ Craftiness
- ☐ Creativity
- ☐ Credibility
- ☐ Curiosity
- ☐ Daring
- ☐ Decisiveness
- ☐ Delight

- ☐ Dependability
- ☐ Depth
- ☐ Desire
- ☐ Determination
- ☐ Devotion
- ☐ Devoutness
- ☐ Dignity
- ☐ Diligence
- ☐ Direction
- ☐ Directness
- ☐ Discipline
- ☐ Discovery
- ☐ Discretion
- ☐ Diversity
- ☐ Dominance
- ☐ Dreaming
- ☐ Drive
- ☐ Duty
- ☐ Eagerness
- ☐ Ease
- ☐ Economy
- ☐ Ecstasy
- ☐ Education
- ☐ Effectiveness
- ☐ Efficiency
- ☐ Elation
- ☐ Elegance
- ☐ Empathy
- ☐ Encouragement
- ☐ Endurance
- ☐ Energy

- ☐ Enjoyment
- ☐ Entertainment
- ☐ Enthusiasm
- ☐ Environmentalism
- ☐ Ethics
- ☐ Euphoria
- ☐ Excellence
- ☐ Excitement
- ☐ Exhilaration
- ☐ Expectancy
- ☐ Experience
- ☐ Expertise
- ☐ Exploration
- ☐ Expressiveness
- ☐ Extravagance
- ☐ Extroversion
- ☐ Exuberance
- ☐ Fairness
- ☐ Faith
- ☐ Fame
- ☐ Family
- ☐ Fascination
- ☐ Fashion
- ☐ Fearlessness
- ☐ Ferocity
- ☐ Fidelity
- ☐ Fierceness
- ☐ Finances
- ☐ Firmness
- ☐ Fitness
- ☐ Flexibility

- ☐ Flow
- ☐ Focus
- ☐ Fortitude
- ☐ Frankness
- ☐ Freedom
- ☐ Friendship
- ☐ Frugality
- ☐ Fun
- ☐ Generosity
- ☐ Giving
- ☐ Grace
- ☐ Gratitude
- ☐ Growth
- ☐ Guidance
- ☐ Happiness
- ☐ Harmony
- ☐ Health
- ☐ Heart
- ☐ Helpfulness
- ☐ Heroism
- ☐ Holiness
- ☐ Honesty
- ☐ Honor
- ☐ Hopefulness
- ☐ Hospitality
- ☐ Humility
- ☐ Humor
- ☐ Hygiene
- ☐ Imagination
- ☐ Impact
- ☐ Impartiality

- ☐ Independence
- ☐ Individuality
- ☐ Industry
- ☐ Influence
- ☐ Ingenuity
- ☐ Inquisitiveness
- ☐ Insightfulness
- ☐ Inspiration
- ☐ Integrity
- ☐ Intelligence
- ☐ Intensity
- ☐ Intimacy
- ☐ Introspection
- ☐ Intuition
- ☐ Investing
- ☐ Involvement
- ☐ Joy
- ☐ Justice
- ☐ Keenness
- ☐ Kindness
- ☐ Knowledge
- ☐ Leadership
- ☐ Learning
- ☐ Liberation
- ☐ Lightness
- ☐ Liveliness
- ☐ Logic
- ☐ Longevity
- ☐ Love
- ☐ Loyalty
- ☐ Making a difference

- ☐ Marriage
- ☐ Mastery
- ☐ Maturity
- ☐ Meaning
- ☐ Meekness
- ☐ Mellowness
- ☐ Meticulousness
- ☐ Mindfulness
- ☐ Modesty
- ☐ Motivation
- ☐ Mysteriousness
- ☐ Nature
- ☐ Neatness
- ☐ Nerve
- ☐ Nonconformity
- ☐ Obedience
- ☐ Open-mindedness
- ☐ Optimism
- ☐ Order
- ☐ Organization
- ☐ Originality
- ☐ Outdoors
- ☐ Outlandishness
- ☐ Outrageousness
- ☐ Partnership
- ☐ Patience
- ☐ Passion
- ☐ Peace
- ☐ Perceptiveness
- ☐ Perfection
- ☐ Perkiness

☐ Perseverance	☐ Relaxation
☐ Persistence	☐ Reliability
☐ Persuasiveness	☐ Relief
☐ Philanthropy	☐ Religiousness
☐ Playfulness	☐ Reputation
☐ Pleasantness	☐ Resilience
☐ Pleasure	☐ Resolution
☐ Poise	☐ Resolve
☐ Popularity	☐ Resourcefulness
☐ Potency	☐ Respect
☐ Power	☐ Responsibility
☐ Practicality	☐ Rest
☐ Pragmatism	☐ Restraint
☐ Precision	☐ Reverence
☐ Preparedness	☐ Richness
☐ Presence	☐ Sacredness
☐ Pride	☐ Sacrifice
☐ Privacy	☐ Saintliness
☐ Proactivity	☐ Satisfaction
☐ Professionalism	☐ Science
☐ Prosperity	☐ Security
☐ Prudence	☐ Self-control
☐ Punctuality	☐ Selflessness
☐ Purity	☐ Self-reliance
☐ Rationality	☐ Self-respect
☐ Realism	☐ Sensitivity
☐ Reason	☐ Sensuality
☐ Recognition	☐ Serenity
☐ Recreation	☐ Service
☐ Refinement	☐ Sexiness
☐ Reflection	☐ Sexuality

- ☐ Sharing
- ☐ Shrewdness
- ☐ Silence
- ☐ Silliness
- ☐ Simplicity
- ☐ Sincerity
- ☐ Skillfulness
- ☐ Solidarity
- ☐ Solitude
- ☐ Sophistication
- ☐ Soundness
- ☐ Speed
- ☐ Spirit
- ☐ Spirituality
- ☐ Spontaneity
- ☐ Stability
- ☐ Status
- ☐ Stealth
- ☐ Stillness
- ☐ Strength
- ☐ Structure
- ☐ Success
- ☐ Support
- ☐ Surprise
- ☐ Sympathy
- ☐ Teaching
- ☐ Teamwork
- ☐ Thankfulness
- ☐ Thoroughness
- ☐ Thoughtfulness
- ☐ Thriftiness

- ☐ Tidiness
- ☐ Traditionalism
- ☐ Tranquility
- ☐ Transcendence
- ☐ Trust
- ☐ Truth
- ☐ Understanding
- ☐ Unflappability
- ☐ Uniqueness
- ☐ Unity
- ☐ Usefulness
- ☐ Variety
- ☐ Victory
- ☐ Vigor
- ☐ Virtue
- ☐ Vision
- ☐ Vitality
- ☐ Vivacity
- ☐ Volunteering
- ☐ Warm-heartedness
- ☐ Watchfulness
- ☐ Wealth
- ☐ Willfulness
- ☐ Willingness
- ☐ Winning
- ☐ Wisdom
- ☐ Wittiness
- ☐ Wonder
- ☐ Worthiness
- ☐ Youthfulness
- ☐ Zeal

2. Take a moment to think about what matters most to you in your life as you look at your top five values from the exercise above. Now ask yourself *(honestly)* if these values support your pursuit of happiness or if they tend to move you into the feeling of duty, obligation or stress. If you recall from our relaxation chapter, there can be no true happiness or lasting inner peace when the Amygdala is triggered. At the same time, raising awareness of this situation creates the opportunity for you to diffuse the fear, and release yourself from the hold that the Amygdala has placed on you.

   Now, as you allow yourself to relax and breathe deeply, ask yourself if there is a way to alter this value or its associated belief in order to support all of your needs.

3. Now I invite you to notice if there are any values on your list that are contradictory. Is it time to let go of the hold that these past beliefs have on you? You can use the exercise in the extended version of this chapter to easily do this.
   Is it time to move forward into a new part of your life that is based on the values of kindness, compassion and true caring for not only others but for yourself as well? If a part of you feels the need to justify self-care and nurturing, that's easy to accomplish. You simply need to assure yourself that this is a necessary part of self-responsibility.

   By taking care of yourself and your own needs, you release others from having to do this *for* you.

O... OBSTACLES

"Being happy doesn't mean everything is perfect.
It means you've decided to look beyond the
imperfections."

--- Devon Dashelle Wesley

Kaizenized Quick Notes

- *Many times we believe that one thing is holding us back while in actuality it is something entirely different. By relaxing, and moving out of the place of fear and judgment, we can explore the truth about these obstacles in a clearer way. As a result we exponentially increase our chances of experiencing happiness, success and inner peace.*

- *By understanding that obstacles are merely blocks in energy caused by unhelpful beliefs and subconscious programming, we can create a level of detachment that enables us to release ourselves from the emotional charge that has been keeping us stuck.*

- *Repressing negative emotions while forcing ourselves to think positive thoughts in an attempt to be happy, only produces watered-down temporary results at best. Eventually, we become like a clogged up drain, filled with the waste and debris of all that we do not want to see or feel. In time we find that nothing flows through our lives easily. Everything becomes difficult and tense, and as a result we become very UNhappy.*

- *Feeling negativity, sadness, grief, shame, guilt and vulnerability does not kill our chances to feel happiness. In fact, by acknowledging these feelings and allowing them to flow through us without resistance, we increase our ability to keep our hearts open to happiness.*

- *Fear and discomfort are only temporary. Everyone experiences these feelings at some time or another. Repressing these emotions creates more suffering than if we were to choose to face them and allow them to flow through naturally without resistance.*

- *The Amygdala closes the doors of the mind, causing us to run around in circles searching for answers that never come. While reacting to fear based on survival instincts, and negative memories, we are subject to the effects of our subconscious programming. The use of Kaizen small questions posed in a simple way helps to relax the Amygdala, allowing it to go back to sleep while it opens the doors to our creative resources once again.*

The Extended Version

What is really standing in your way?

In the last chapters we explored how our values are often tied to unconscious beliefs that create discomfort. This is turn triggers the Amygdala and keeps us stuck in a repetitive cycle of limitations and fear.

We also explored how it is possible to think that we want one thing in particular, when really it is something much richer that we are yearning for. Until we dig a little deeper and uncover this essence, we will find ourselves continually coming up short in the area of happiness, true success, and inner peace.

We also explored how tension and fear, caused by moving out of our comfort zone and routines, triggers the Amygdala, which then closes us off from our creative resources and cognitive thinking. In effect, it minimizes our ability to identify the opportunities that are available to us.

As you can see, we have already covered a significant amount of information that you can use to experience more happiness in your life. Yet without exploring your obstacles, you would still, most likely, continue *to* find yourself on the short end of the happiness stick.

So what *else* might be standing in *your* way?

...Much more than you are consciously aware of at the moment. Thankfully, that is about to change as we take a closer look at the subconscious mind and how we can work with it consciously in order to move beyond challenges, blocks and limitations in an easy, natural, and progressive way.

The Subconscious Mind

90% of everything we experience on a daily basis is based on subconscious programming. Memories and impressions from the past continue to affect us today in ways that we are far too often unaware of.

From the moment we are born, until the last breath we take, the subconscious mind is busily recording EVERYTHING that we experience. This occurs whether we are aware of it or not. Unfortunately, many of these recordings are often based on a lack of knowledge and maturity at the time the experience took place. Because of this, misunderstandings were created resulting in unnecessary hardships, fears, and limiting beliefs. These recordings, once established, began to repeat again and again, each time compounding, growing stronger, denser, and more convincing.

Like a horse travelling around and around on a carousel, we are tethered to this subconscious programming, unaware of what's actually happening. This habitual cycle of repetition continues, until something happens to temporarily break the connection - if only for a brief moment. In this instant of increased awareness, something within us is triggered and in a flash we realize that we DO have a choice. It IS POSSIBLE to do things differently. WE CAN BREAK FREE! The fact that you're reading this book right now, and have gotten this far in the process, is a pretty good indication that you are ready to untether yourself and jump off your carousel!

There was a silly meme making its way around the Internet recently. It said, *"I don't make the same mistake twice. I make it five or six times, just to be sure."*

I can certainly relate to this! How about you? Have you ever found yourself saying, *"Why did I do that (or say that) again? I should know better by now!"* Chances are, you were just caught in the reactionary rut of an old subconscious program. The sad fact is, this reaction is going to happen again and again and again until you realize what is happening.

Awareness is the key to uncovering those tricky obstacles neatly tucked away in your psyche. By simply paying attention to the moment, to what you are experiencing, feeling, and thinking, you can stop the unconscious cycles of habitual reaction by *choosing your actions consciously.*

The best part about this process of mindfulness and choice is that each tiny step goes a long way. Like an intricate maze of dominoes standing on end, you only need to tip over one single tile to achieve a cascading effect! And even though you have an immeasurable number of subconscious programs that affect you on a daily basis, by simply making **one conscious change** in your day, an effect can be created that touches all parts of your life in the most profound and beautiful way.

Of course, there are ways to make this process even more beneficial. As mentioned earlier, relaxation is most definitely one of the major keys. Without a level of relaxation there can be no choice. There is only reaction based on fear, past memories and the survival instinct. The first step to creating conscious choice is to breathe and use the relaxation methods that best suit you.

The next step is to enter into the place where these programs are stored; the subconscious mind. How do you do this? To start with, it is helpful to learn the language of the subconscious mind.

Earlier I mentioned that every *word* and every *thing* is merely a symbol for something deeper. Each symbol represents an essence of something greater. While logic and analytical thinking belong to the conscious mind, recorded sensations, stories, impressions and feelings belong to the subconscious mind in the form of symbols. Sights, sounds, intuitive nudges, scents, tastes and physical feelings represent far more than one could imagine… just as a picture is worth a thousands words, so too is any impression from our other senses. This is especially true when they are experienced inwardly, like a dream, or a recalled memory, both of which are working directly through the subconscious mind in some way.

Each experience we have ever had has been recorded in absolute detail by way of the various symbols mentioned above. Although completely accurate at the time of the event, these subconscious recordings are often incomplete in conscious understanding based on inexperience and immaturity at the time they were created. This is where the problem lies.

For example, let's explore what might have occurred if you were bit by a dog when you when you were very young...

- You may have grown up with a fear of dogs.

- You may have developed a belief that all dogs are dangerous.

- Or you may have realized that only some dogs bite, and while it is important to use care when approaching unfamiliar animals, most dogs are actually quite loving and gentle.

You certainly might have become trapped on the carousel of subconscious belief based on the first two answers if you did not have the opportunity to see the truth in the situation.

You most *definitely* would have become trapped if the experience were compounded by intense emotion, such as witnessing your mother reacting in fear. If you saw her crying or screaming at the dog and the owner, this would have told your subconscious mind to pay attention BIG TIME! Immediately it would have known that this event was a doozy. It would have made sure that you never forgot that dogs = danger. The Amygdala would have been connected in this experience as well and from that point on, whenever a dog crossed your path, BAM! The fear center within your brain would be triggered in a profound way. The same process of subconscious recording and compounding based on the level of emotion present in the experience is true when it comes to other beliefs, memories and impressions that we experience on a regular basis as well. If we are repetitively shown that the world is a sad, lonely and dangerous place, through our exposure to news articles, songs, TV shows, books, and movies, our subconscious mind will register this as truth and we will react accordingly. Perhaps you've heard the saying: *where your attention lies, that is where you will be.* This is precisely what I'm talking about. Just as it is important to watch what you wish for, it is also important to watch what you are paying attention to on a repetitive basis. Thankfully, this also works in a positive way. If we want to change our subconscious programming in order to live life in a happier, more successful and peaceful way, we simply need to repetitively choose to focus on the things that support this state of being.

Kaizen small questions can open doors

You already know that Kaizen small steps can help to create success in a way that does not trigger the fear center in the brain. You also know that each small step compounds, creating greater and greater levels of success as each builds upon the other, creating momentum at a comfortable pace. Perhaps, by this point, you have experienced firsthand how this gentle technique is a wonderful way to move beyond the deep-seated subconscious programs that cause us to feel overwhelmed or afraid. Hopefully you have realized by now that by keeping the steps small, you will continue to unfold and grow in the way that you choose to: easily, naturally and by choice rather than default programming.

Now, I'd like to share with you what Kaizen small questions can do when it comes to overcoming subconscious programs. But first, I've got a question for you. How can you possibly fix something if you don't know it's broken? Second, to follow up that question, I would like to clarify the fact that in no way are *you* broken, nor have you ever been broken. What may be broken is simply the *connection* that you have with the deeper part of yourself. But this is only temporary. There is an easy fix for this! But before we can fix it, we need to investigate the situation a little more deeply. So go ahead and put on your detective cap, get out your magnifying glass and let's go exploring.

- *Why does this always happen to me?*
- *Why can't I do anything right?*
- *Why am I always so unhappy?*

Do any of these questions sound familiar? My guess is that you've uttered at least one of them at some point in your life. Maybe more? Come on... honesty check here. The truth is most of us have said *all* of these things. I'll bet that if you *have* asked these questions, then you, like the rest of us, soon discovered the answers in a very undesirable way, by receiving yet another experience that served to compound and solidify these thoughts.

The mind is an amazing tool. It thrives on questions and will not stop searching until it finds the answer and gives it to us in precisely the way that we asked for it. For example, if you were to ask the question, *"What is wrong with me?"* the mind would immediately begin to chew on this question and in turn would remind you of all the negative self-talk that you've repeated to yourself over the years along with all of the criticism that you've ever received, or *think* that you've received. Yes, you would get the answer to your question, but is this answer really what you want? Is it really going to be helpful for you?

How about this question, *"Why can't I just be happy?"* I ask you to think about this carefully now. Are you absolutely certain that you would like to learn even more ways why you *can't* be happy? Because if you continue to ask this question enough times, you'll certainly find out. But truthfully, wouldn't you prefer to discover ways to choose to be happy instead?

Okay, chances are you are well practiced in the art of asking lousy questions that produce lousy results. Join the club! We've all had our fair share of practice. But fear not! Remember the power of opposites that we talked about in the beginning of this book? In this case it comes down to this:

First...

Knowing what to do often begins by learning what *not* to do.

Second...

Stop asking negative questions.

...unless, you enjoy receiving negative answers. Instead, how about posing your questions in a way that will bring you the information that you can use proactively? Now, let's take the list of questions above and turn them around to our advantage:

- *Why might this be happening **for** me?*
- *What am I doing **right**?*
- *What is **one small step** that I **can** take in order to*
  ***create more happiness** in my life **right now**?*

Can you sense the difference in energy between the two sets of questions? Can you feel how the first set of negative questions would be guaranteed to produce negative answers? Can you sense the feeling of negative energy in yourself as you read each one? How could we ever expect positive results from such a negative frame of mind? Did you notice how the second set of questions had a much different feeling to it? Could you sense the creative energy present in this group? Could you feel the sense of possibility and positive energy as you read each one? These are the types of questions that will result in positive answers and in turn will get you to where you *want* to be... positively!

At this point in the journey you might be saying, "But I've asked positive questions in the past, and I did not receive any positive answers. In fact I did not receive *any* answers at all!" Fair enough. I can relate. There can be a number of reasons for this experience. First, the question you asked may have been too big. This can result in a couple of things. First, there may be so many possible answers that the mind just kept circling in on itself as it discovered more and more possibilities. At this point you may have felt a sense of distrust in the answers that you were receiving, being that there was not ONE SINGLE RIGHT ANSWER. You may have started to second guess yourself as a result of this. Ringing any bells here? Secondly, big questions with a lot of possibilities for answers can create a level of discomfort within us. Remember what happens when we move beyond our comfort zone too far. You've got it. The Amygdala is triggered again. There is no chance of any answers coming through when this happens. So what is the best way to get around this?

Keep your questions small and simple.

It's better to ask many small questions and receive many small answers than it is to ask the BIGGIES and come up with nothing. Notice that in the third question of the positive list I wrote:

"What is **one small step** that I **can** take in order to **create**

112

more happiness in my life **right now**?" rather than asking... "How can I be happy?"

The first question is a Kaizen small question: simple and positive. It does not demand detailed answers or intricate plans. It also limits the answer to ONE SMALL STEP and clarifies the time that we want to be happy as NOW. Sounds pretty clear, doesn't it? The second question, "How can I be happy?" allows for far too many angles, answers, timeframes and methods. There is so much information that could be provided, and as a result the mind could continue to chew on this question throughout all eternity, spitting out little bits of info here and there in a way that would never provide us with an absolute answer. Part of the reason for this is because the mind would also be conveying the fact that none of the answers being provided was completely the "*right*" one. In turn, we would automatically second guess ourselves due to this incomplete feeling. By providing a frame to work within, however, we make it much simple for the mind to provide us with what we want and need in a way that feels clear and complete in the moment.

Another reason why you may not have received an answer to a question that you have asked is that although you may have posed the question in a simplified form, you might *not* have provided a way to *receive* the answer. Or you may have just stopped listening for the answer. Believe me when I say that I don't mean for this to offend you. It's pretty common for each of us to ask questions and then close our ears when the answer we receive is not what we wanted to hear. We don't stop listening on purpose. *Well*, maybe *sometimes* we do. But for the most part it just happens. That is, until we consciously choose to provide a way for the answers to come through; one that allows us to hear clearly and to understand without resistance. There are many ways to do this. One of my favorite ways is to ask my Kaizen small question right before going to sleep. Then upon rising I quickly take note of my dreams. More often than not the answer is there, when I wake. Sometimes I receive the answer right away, while other times it's necessary to ask repetitively night after night for a couple of weeks or so. The trick, I've found, is to just keep asking. Remember, the mind will not give up its search until it finds the answer to the questions that we ask repetitively, and thankfully it will keep giving us the answer until we successfully receive it. So no worries - you will get your answer if you're listening. And if you do happen to miss it on the first round, the answer will come around again and again until you do get it.

Finally, one more reason why you may not have received an answer to your question is because the time might not be right... *yet*. Sometimes it can actually be quite a blessing to *not* receive what we ask for, at least not *when* we ask for it, or in the *way* that we ask for it. Trusting, even just a little bit, that you are receiving exactly what you need when you need it, can make life far easier and more relaxed in every way. It can release us from tension and stress while it allows us to accept, in a positively helpful way, whatever is happening in a given moment. The bonus to trusting the process of life as it unfolds, without engaging in unnecessary worry, is that all of a sudden we often find we are able to smile a little more. We also find that no matter what might be happening, it is always possible to find a little bit of happiness in our day. Who says that life has to be perfect in order for us to experience happiness? And who says that we need to deny that "bad" things happen in life in order to feel happy?

...not me!

Have you been plugging up the sink?

My kids have been doing dishes since they were quite little; it's one of the little ways I've chosen to teach them team work and responsibility. Of course, there have been more than a few broken dishes over the years., which is no biggie, for the most part. But more than that, there have been *quite* a few plugged up sinks!

Although they don't seem to mind washing the plates before they put them in the dishwasher, they don't like to pick up the little bits of food that fall into the sink. Apparently, to them, it feels "icky." So what happens to the icky bits that no one wants to touch? Well, they get stuffed down the drain, of course.

"See, Mom! The sink is all clean!" ..But is it really?

Now, if this were a one shot deal every now and then, it wouldn't be a big thing, but when it happens night after night on a repetitive basis, eventually the bits of food begin to build up. Very quickly the water begins to drain slower and slower and eventually stops altogether. With too many icky bits in the drain, nothing is getting through!

Time for some drain cleaner!

Just like the icky bits of food in the clogged up sink, negative thoughts, emotions and memories that we stuff down inside ourselves have a way of blocking us up too. When this happens, there is little to no happiness that can flow through. When it comes down to it, experiences and emotions - whether positive or negative - are simply a form of energy.

E-motion = energy in motion. It's as simple as that.

Whether this energy is experienced as positive or negative depends on the judgment that we decide to place upon it at the time it is experienced. More often than not, this is done on a completely reactionary basis as a result of those old subconscious programs, values and beliefs that we talked about earlier. Understanding this can be helpful in many ways, but it can also be a double-edged sword if we fall into the trap of denial and repression in the name of "positivity." With all of the talk today about the law of attraction, and the fact that thoughts become things, many have taken this to mean that we must *never* allow ourselves to think, feel or experience *anything* negatively. Unfortunately, what this has resulted in is a whole lot of suffering by stuffing down the icky bits within ourselves, rather than dealing with them properly.

Sickness, disease, emotional issues, and neuroses: each one of these is a state that has been created by the clogged drains inside of us. Pockets of energy in the form of icky feelings, negative thoughts, and memories that we just don't want to touch: they do not disappear on their own. Instead, they build up until we come to the point in our lives when happiness, success and inner peace no longer flow freely. Eventually, through the continual repression of undesirable feelings, positivity will no longer flow through our lives to any significant degree. If this is happening to you, I have one suggestion to make:

Better get out the drain cleaner!

There are many different *brands* of energy cleaner to choose from. In fact, there is something for *every* kind of clog that you might be experiencing. Some of these *cleaners* include the following:

- Kaizen Creative NLP

- Emotional Freedom technique (EFT)
- Tai Chi, Qi Gong, Reiki or any of the other various forms of energy movement techniques
- Visualization, mantras or any technique that allows you to relax and raise your level of awareness in a way that can help you to face the undesirable and finally allow it to be cleared away

But why wait until we're backed up completely by fear, guilt, shame, anger, sadness, grief, jealousy, or any of the other feelings we deem undesirable? By allowing ourselves to acknowledge what we are feeling at the time we are feeling it, without repressing anything, it is far easier for us to move through difficult situations and come out on the other side smiling again. This doesn't mean we allow ourselves to wallow in the discomfort or hold on to the pain. In fact, by shining a light on our feelings, identifying them, and facing them head on, these feelings often begin to lose their power over us naturally. Thankfully, there are many avenues for support in this area as well. We do not have to face our feelings alone. If we need help, there are options available, but this can only be helpful if we ask.

Creative Exploration

1. Kaizen Small Questions

Focusing on questions that can show us what is working in our lives, and what we *do* have going for us in the moment, puts us into a more empowered state. In this position, we are better able to identify our challenges and work through them in a positive way. With a little bit of optimism and clarity, we may find it much easier to explore our situation from a higher perspective. Rather than looking at why something is happening *to* us, we can easily shift to the outlook of why something is happening *for* us. The following are some powerful Kaizen small questions that you might choose to use as you begin exploring your own challenges in a deeper, more helpful way:

- What CAN I do right here and now?
- What resources are present in my life already?
- How can I break down my current goal or situation into smaller, more manageable steps?
- How can I break these steps down even more in order to bring them to the point where success is guaranteed?

2. Identifying Symbols As Triggers

By raising our level of awareness with respect to the things that make us feel uncomfortable, we can begin to take back our power of choice. In any given moment we can choose to act differently, but only when we realize what is happening.

The following are some Kaizen small questions that can help you to identify your triggers:

- What is setting me off right now?
- How is this making me feel in this moment?
- What do my triggers look like, sound like, smell like, taste like, and feel like today?
- How would I normally REACT in this situation?
- How can I choose to ACT differently?

3. Digging Deeper

Often people automatically accept the outer representation of a perceived obstacle as the obvious truth. They think that a particular thing or situation is standing in their way, but in actuality this obstacle, more often than not, is merely a symbol for a challenge that exists much deeper.

In the following example you will see how particular questions can be used to raise awareness as to what and where the true challenge lies. In this example I'll use a very typical problem that many are currently facing: the belief that financial difficulty is the cause of unhappiness. In an attempt to dig deeper into this widespread belief and gain a greater perspective of the situation, numerous people, from many areas of the world, and from many walks of life, were asked to describe their experience and opinion. The majority of those that I spoke to reported that their financial challenges are a direct result of the following:

- A job that does not pay well enough
- The cost of living is too high
- They have far too much debt to pay

The general consensus from those polled is, *"If only I had more money, then most if not all of my troubles would go away."* But in truth, the challenge lies much deeper than their job, bills, debt, or even *money* in a general sense. This raises some questions:

- What is *really* causing this financial challenge?

- How deep do we have to dig in order to uncover the true reason for these difficulties?

By exploring our individual levels of consciousness we find it easy to discover the answers. In order to begin this process of unearthing the truth from within, we need to do the following:

First, it is important to identify the outer symbol that represents the challenge we are facing. In this case the symbol is:

Financial difficulty

Second, we must take a look at how our various levels of experience and awareness may be affecting our financial situation.

In this case the levels of experience are represented in the following:

ENVIRONMENT:

Low paying job

Cost of living is too high

Too much personal debt

BEHAVIORS AND EMOTIONS:

Retail therapy *(Buying things in order to feel better)*

Stressed, closed off from creative resources

CAPABILITIES, STRATEGIES and SKILLS:

Insufficient training and inexperience

Limited job search

BELIEFS and VALUES:

Believe that life is a struggle

Value hard work and sacrifice above happiness

Believe that they are not worthy of abundance

IDENTITY:

Feeling self as only human

Family has always struggled

Feeling less worthy and/or less valued than others

SPIRITUAL VIEWPOINT, PURPOSE or MISSION IN LIFE:

Unclear, disappointment, limited success in connection

Why am I here?

What is this life really all about?

Through the example above you can see that there is much more to this challenge than initially meets the eye. The financial struggle that they have been experiencing is merely a symptom or a symbol of a deeper challenge that is occurring within. By exploring this symbol in greater detail it is easy to see why these people continue to struggle.

Imagine for a moment what might happen if these individuals shifted their thinking in the following way. What if:

- Each individual saw themselves as a conscious creative being whose mission was to live life richly and fully, to thrive and to create happiness in ways that would benefit others, as well as themselves, in their receiving.

- Each individual believed that change was possible, opportunities were present, and that they were not limited to the way things appeared to be now, or the way things have always been.
- Each individual was able to relax and tap into his or her creative resources in ways that helped him or her to find unique ways to gain the experience, training and budgeting skills necessary to achieve their goals and desires.
- Each individual saw life as an opportunity to experience things in a unique way rather than being limited to the way that society deemed things to be.

Now that you have read through the list above, notice how the shift in perspective has made *you* feel? Can you feel a change in yourself and your beliefs as well?

If you are experiencing challenges in your own life, you might find the categories for exploration above to be helpful. In order to take advantage of this experience you might start by answering the following questions:

1. What challenges are present in my life? What symbols or symptoms do these challenges choose to take?

   Note: Health, finances, and relationships are the three most common symbols of blocked energy most of us experience.

2. What physical or environmental symptoms are present?

3. How do I behave when I am faced with this challenge? How do

my triggers make me feel emotionally? How is this situation affecting my actions and emotions?

4. What skills do I have that can help me to move out of or through this challenge? What additional skills or resources would be helpful for me?

5. What beliefs and values do I have regarding this situation? Are these beneficial or harmful? Is there a new perspective that I can take in order to see things more clearly?

6. How do I identify myself in this situation? How do I identify myself generally? Am I giving myself enough credit? Is my self-confidence and self-worth as strong as it could be? What changes can I make to help improve my sense of identity (even a little bit to start)?

7. How do I view myself spiritually? Am I aware of my mission in life? Am I in alignment with my dreams? Am I taking small steps toward making my dreams a reality? Do I have a sense of purpose in my life? Do my answers to the questions above support this purpose? Do my actions reflect my dreams?

Some of the happiest people have very few things, but have so much more than any money can buy!

Unknown

By letting go of our insatiable desire to fix and change everyone and everything around us, we give ourselves the space to focus our attention on the true source of our own happiness, success, and fulfillment... Ourselves!

Rashida Rowe

L... LEVERAGE SUCCESS

Our happiness depends on the habit of mind we
cultivate. So practice happy thinking every day.
Cultivate the merry heart, develop the happiness habit,
and life will become a continual feast.

-- Norman Vincent Peale

Kaizenized Quick Notes

- *Focusing on gratitude acknowledges a level of success that you have already achieved. By focusing on what you are thankful for, you in turn create favorable conditions that encourage even more happiness and success to flow into your life, bringing with it much more to be grateful for.*

- *By focusing on past success along with the methods that you used to achieve your success, you provide yourself with powerful information. You become aware of tools and techniques that have helped you in the past, w h i c h may also help you to create even more success today.*

- *By exploring the habits, behaviors, values and beliefs of other happy individuals, you can use this information in your own life to create even more happiness for yourself.*

- *By imagining the successful outcome of a desire, through the art of creative visualization, in a way that allows you to act as if it has already manifested in the present tense, you ignite powerful creative forces within yourself. These forces then set off a domino effect that naturally carries this imagined scenario into a true state of being. In other words, thoughts do become things when you use a success frame of mind and mentality in the act of imaging.*

- *Successful imaging can occur in both positive and negative visualizations. While it is important to watch the thoughts and emotions that you are experiencing, it is equally as important to avoid repressing anything that you feel. As long as you make a point to tip the scales on the side of positivity as often as possible, you will experience greater happiness, success and inner peace.*

The Extended Version

What does it mean to succeed?

Before we can create any level of true success in our lives, it is important to first understand what success means to us personally. How about *you*? Do you think you know what success means? Are you sure? Before you set that thought in stone, you might want to think again.

"He has achieved success who has

lived well,

laughed often,

and loved much..."

Bessie Anderson Stanley

So often in our lives we take for granted the simple things, like the meaning of a word that we have used repetitively throughout our lives. Most of the time, after we initially learn the dictionary meaning of a word, we rarely consider it again. By doing so, in a sense we've actually allowed another person or group to create a recorded program in our subconscious mind. This happens all the time and for the most part it's fairly harmless, or so it may seem.

The interesting thing, is that when we take a moment to look at the word in a deeper way, we often find there is much more to it than that which initially meets the eye. There is definitely much more to each symbol or word than the dictionary can ever state, especially when we apply it to our own lives in a personal way.

One method I like to use when digging deeper into the meaning of something, whether outside of myself or within, is **the fast forward/rewind technique**. Used to specifically discover the true meaning of authentic success, it would go a little like this:

Part I - Fast forward to any time in the future.

Remember to allow yourself to relax a little as you begin this technique. By doing so you will find yourself tapping into your creative resources with greater ease. As you relax, allow yourself to see, hear, sense, smell and taste as much as you can in an inward sense by connecting with the imagination. By doing so you will be working with your subconscious mind in a way that can successfully create some very wonderful changes in your life today.

So now if you're ready, let's get started.

Go ahead, get comfortable and...

B...r...e...a...t...h...e...

Imagine for a moment that you have, in fact, achieved success in an authentic sense. What does a day in your successful life look like to you? Remember to engage as many senses as possible in the form of sights, sounds, feelings, intuitive nudges, tastes and scents.

Speaking in present tense terms, how would you describe this experience of success?

- Would you say you are successful because you are accomplishing your goals?
- Or is success more of a feeling of satisfaction that you are experiencing?
- Have you accumulated a lot of money or material goods? Is this how you are measuring your success?
- Or have you achieved this successful state by overcoming a challenge in some way?
- What words would you use to describe how you feel?

Go ahead, whenever you're ready.

Check all that apply:

☐ Confident	☐ Productive
☐ Strong	☐ Calm
☐ Resilient	☐ Relaxed
☐ Blessed	☐ Alive
☐ Grateful	☐ Appreciated

Isn't it interesting to see how many different ways we can view success? Sounds a little bit like happiness in this way, doesn't it? In fact I wonder if we might even venture to say that success is a measure of true happiness? They do seem to go hand in hand, don't they? But once again we come to the question:

Which came first:

The chicken or the egg?

Success or true happiness?

To discover the answer to this question, we must explore the second part of the technique...

Part II - Time to rewind.

By retracing your steps from the point of experienced success to the present moment, you will find that you are able to pick up some very valuable, helpful information that you can use here and now to experience a richer sense of success today. In order to gain a greater sense of clarity, it can be helpful to focus on a few particular points in this process. In a moment we will go through each one of these key points individually. As you do this, I invite you to sit back, relax and connect with your creative resources a little more deeply. Remember to...

Breathe, relax and imagine

Point one:

Picture yourself rising up now from the point of success that you have been visiting. Floating up, higher and higher, allow yourself to take on a perspective from a place above the *successful* scene. Notice what you look like down there: happy and at peace. What other qualities do you see in your appearance and in your energy?

Next, allow yourself to continue floating back toward the present day. Do so *very* slowly, as you continue to pay attention to events that occur along the timeline on this journey.

Now, bring yourself to the moment in time, just before your experience of true success materialized. Ask yourself what you were feeling just before you struck this success.

Most people I have shared this technique with report a sensation of immense gratitude and anticipation along with a strong sense of knowing just before they experienced success. To each one it felt like a solid, assured feeling, balanced, strong and secure, while at the same time they also experienced a sensation of being lighthearted and weightless.

Note: This, experience, however, in a number of cases, was preceded by the feeling of immense doubt and fear along with a dogged sense of determination to see things through to their completion, no matter what that completion turned out to be.

How about you? What do you notice yourself sensing, on this imaginative journey, at the point just before success strikes your life?

Point two:

Once again, slowly moving back along the timeline...

Notice the people who have played a part in helping you to create the conditions in your life that have helped you to achieve authentic success, true happiness and inner peace. These people can be *anyone* from the past or present. You might know these people personally, or you may have only heard of them, read about them or may have seen them on the screen. These helpful individuals can be fictional or real, celebrities, or family. They can even be imagined entirely. No matter who these people may be, they all have at least *one* thing in common. They have influenced your success in some way. Perhaps they too were successful in their own right. Perhaps they exuded a quality you admire, like self-confidence, patience, creativity, wisdom or resourcefulness among a myriad of other qualities.

What I invite you to do at this point is to simply notice what each person contributed to your personal journey. Then notice the energy or quality they embody that speaks of success, happiness and inner peace.

As you look at these helpful people, notice the way that they conduct themselves, notice their posture and the expression on their faces. Pay attention to the activities that they engage in, along with the energy that they radiate. You may see their energy shining like a light all around them, or coming from them, from the core of their being. Notice what color this energy is and how it makes you feel. Notice as much as you can about each individual. Then breathe in this experience. Feel the energy of success, happiness and true inner peace that is present in this experience. Feel this energy beginning to grow inside of you.

Allow yourself to feel the positive energy from each of these helpful individuals within every cell of your body. Enjoy the feeling that you are experiencing, and while you're at it, you might like to add a little bit of gratitude as well.

Now realize that *all* of this energy and *all* of these positive qualities actually belong to you! They always have! The truth is, it is impossible to feel something that is not already a part of you. YOU are the successful one, the peaceful one, the wise one, the happy one, the creative one. YOU own all of these qualities that you have admired in others. You were simply seeing them in someone else, rather than yourself. But now you get to embrace each of these powerful qualities in yourself wholeheartedly.

With this sense of accomplishment in your heart, notice how there really is no marked difference between the state of true success, happiness and inner peace. In essence they all boil down to the same thing: an experience that goes beyond words and is far richer than anything the outer eyes can see or the ears can hear. It is something that only the heart and soul can feel.

Point three:

Imagine yourself moving back further and further along the timeline toward the present day. Take note of any details that happen to catch your attention or spark your imagination along the way, including ways to create even more of the "good stuff" in your life.

A successful, happy life, imbued with inner peace, is merely one that is filled with many tiny moments and experiences that have touched your heart in a way that has made you feel thankful for your life in some special way.

What are you grateful for?

Focusing on gratitude acknowledges the fact that you have already achieved a level of success in some particular way. By focusing on the feeling of gratitude, you create favorable conditions that encourage even more success to flow into your life, bringing with it even more to be grateful for. Talk about a win-win situation in every way!

How, then, do you focus on gratitude? Do you write a list of all the things you're grateful for? Do you simply feel it, and then move on? Do record in your journal the special events in your day that caused you to feel thankful in some way? Do you share your gratitude with others? Or is there something else that you do?

No matter what you choose to do to focus on gratitude, there is one additional thing you can add in order to create a richer experience that effectively opens your heart even more. It's quite simple: Pay attention to how you are feeling. I mean *really* pay attention, in detail through your senses, both outwardly as well as within your being. You can start to do this by focusing on the following:

- Notice how the energy of gratitude and true appreciation feels in your body.

- Notice where you are feeling the energy within your body.

- Notice the effect that results from your increased

focus and attention. Is the feeling increasing?

Is it radiating outward touching other areas of your body? Or is it becoming more relaxed and as a result feeling more like a part of yourself in a natural way? Could it be bit of both?

- Can you see the color of this grateful energy? What does it look like? What qualities does this color have?

- Does it have a sound? What do you hear?

- If you cannot see a color or hear a sound, what do you think this grateful energy *might* sound like and look like if you *could* see and hear this energy with greater clarity?

- Does this energy bring to mind any memories within you? What does it remind you of and how else do you feel as you remember these moments?

- Notice any other qualities that might be present in the energy of gratitude. How does it move through your body? Does focusing on your breath influence the energy in any way? Can you make the energy of gratitude grow? Does gratitude have a scent or taste? What else do you notice?

Finally, I would like to ask you to think of a way you might be able to recall this deep sensation of gratitude in those moments when you'd like to feel it again. How might you bring to mind the feeling, along with the sights, sounds and all of the other qualities of gratitude? How can you remind yourself of the experience you had here today?

Remember as you do this exercise, that gratitude naturally leads to true happiness, success and inner peace. Isn't it funny to note how all along so many of us thought that it was the other way around? ...That achieving a sense of happiness, success and inner peace would lead us to a feeling of gratitude? But thankfully, now that we know the truth, we can work with this knowledge in a conscious manner. As a result we can design our lives in the way that we would like them to be. By simply bringing to mind the essence and qualities of grateful energy, we can experience it at will. By allowing ourselves to experience a multisensory memory, we are actually creating the experience within ourselves again, right here and now in the current moment. And we are doing so in a way that will attract even more things to be grateful for.

Now *this* my friend is what I call true creativity!

Creative Exploration

By now you may have sensed a pattern emerging within the pages of this book. Perhaps you noticed this pattern as a repetition of phrases and concepts that appeared to pop up every now and again. Or maybe you felt it as a compounding of ideas. You might have even sensed, at times, that we were revisiting particular points that had already been covered in earlier chapters. Whether subtle or obvious, you may have been aware of a layering sensation. If you did notice any of the above, I would like to congratulate you for paying such close attention. If you didn't notice, however, that's ok. Not everyone does right away. You'll certainly notice now.

By overlapping the ideas in one section with points covered in previous chapters, you were being provided with a way to create a strong foundation of knowledge based upon the fundamental points that are necessary in the process of successfully eliciting happiness from within. The best part about this is this was done in a simple, natural way.

In order to create authentic success, in *any* capacity, repetition is necessary. Through a process of practice or reiteration, we are able to work *with*, rather than against the subconscious mind in order to create lasting change.

As you revisited points, whether consciously or unconsciously, you were creating a sense of familiarity or recognition within your subconscious mind. This allowed you to experience a level of comfort and security with the concepts being presented here. In fact they have seemed second nature to you.

The more that you hear something, or are exposed to something, the more the subconscious mind is willing to accept it as truth rather than resisting it as the unknown or the obscure. This doesn't mean that you need to repeat things in the exact way, over and over again, in order for something to become comfortable. In fact, duplication can often create the opposite effect, as you run the risk of creating boredom instead of familiarity. Boredom, in its own right, has the ability to trigger the Amygdala and create resistance just as easily as fear of the unknown can. Therefore, connecting with key elements, and using them in slightly different ways is your best bet as it contains the greatest qualities of both worlds. Through this process you allow yourself to experience comfort in the familiarity while remaining interested and entertained in the freshness of the focus. With this knowledge in mind, can you see how you might personally use the power of unique repetition to your benefit with respect to creating happiness and authentic success? In the opposite way, yet through the same process, can you also see how watching the same commercials over and over again, or listening to the same negative programming (in any form) repetitively, also allows the information or repetitious concepts to become familiar and more acceptable to you?

The following sets of questions may help you to gain a greater level of clarity with respect to unique repetition. As you will see, with only a slight variance, they too are repetitions of the exercises that are woven into the *extended version* section of this chapter. As you read each question, I invite you to notice how the exercise is making you feel. Pay particular attention to any resistance you might be experiencing, while you also notice any new ideas that rise from the experiences.

1. When you think of the word SUCCESS, what comes to mind for you, initially? How do you define success? Recall a time in your life when you felt successful in some way. Remember how we discovered that true happiness can mean many things to many people. Authentic success is the same. When you recall past successes, what is the essence of energy that is present in your memories? What are the finer qualities of the energy? Can you describe them in detail? What do you see, hear, feel, smell, taste and sense?

2. Now think about other times when you have been successful. What techniques, habits, behavior or practices did you use to achieve this success?

Did you start by relaxing in order to clear your mind and focus more directly? If so, what relaxation techniques worked for you?

- Listening to your favorite relaxing music
- A walk in nature
- Deep, focused breathing
- Meditation
- Ensuring you were well rested by getting enough sleep?

Techniques that have helped you achieve success in the past may prove to be helpful again.

3.   Allow yourself to think of someone, past, present or imagined, who epitomizes the resource state you would like to experience in order to help yourself succeed in this moment. Then ask yourself what makes this person successful. You might explore points such as:

- What beliefs or values does this person hold that helps them to create success?
- What is the expression on their face? Are they relaxed, excited, intrigued, or something else?
- Describe their posture and presence.
- What habits do they have that help them to succeed?
- What other helpful qualities or behaviors do you notice?
- What is the overall feeling you sense from their energy and presence?

As you identify the qualities that you believe help this person to succeed, remember that you cannot feel, see, or identify with qualities that you do not already possess within yourself. You must have some personal knowledge to base your judgment on.

Now, the questions remain:

- In what area of your life are these qualities present?

- How can you allow these qualities and this successful energy to grow within you?

Jot down as many thoughts and feelings that come to you, regardless of their clarity. Rest assured, we will be revisiting this exercise again in a slightly different way in the coming chapters.

"If you keep on saying a single thing to yourself, you are likely to attract it to yourself, dreaming it always, then in a twinkle of an eye, it comes to you."

Michael Bassey Johnson

"All our knowledge begins with the senses, proceeds then to the understanding..."

Immanuel Kant

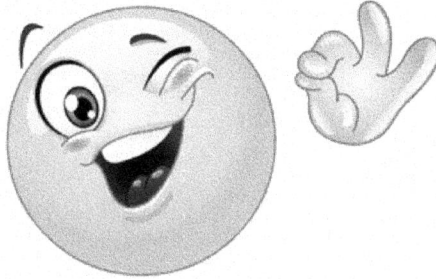

U... UNDERSTANDING

Today I choose life.

Every morning when I wake up I can choose joy, happiness, negativity, pain...

To feel the freedom that comes from being able to continue to make mistakes and choices...

Today I choose to feel life, not to deny my humanity, but embrace it.

-- Kevin Aucoin

Kaizenized Quick Notes

- **Creativity:** *For the majority of people today the word creativity is synonymous with art. The truth is, however, art is merely one form of creative expression. Or, better stated, art is many forms of creative expression under one umbrella. Creativity in and of itself, however, is not art, but rather it is a flow of pure energy that brings an experience to the current moment, which is unique.*

- **Choice:** *The happiest people realize that they always have a choice in each moment and in every experience. They also realize that although not all of their choices are pleasurable, they are still choices that are available to them nevertheless.*

- **Addiction and Self-Sabotage:** *Anything done on a reactionary, repetitive, habitual basis, through an experience that causes us to feel that we have little to no choice can be classified as an addiction. Therefore, repetitive thoughts, along with behaviors, substance use and even relationships can be addictive. The addiction becomes self-sabotage when it prevents us from living life fully, in a way that allows us to grow through rich, uplifting experiences.*

The Extended Version

Redefining Creativity

What is the first thing that comes to mind for you when you see or hear the word creativity? If you're like most people, you might automatically think of art in some form. This is a pretty common response, one that many take for granted, but it can also be quite limiting and sad if you are one who feels left out of this particular category.

Very few people feel comfortable with their artistic talent or skills. In fact, many people claim they do not have one creative bone in their body. Of course, they are generally speaking about art and craftiness when they say this. Thankfully, art itself is *not* creativity; rather, it is one of the many forms of *expression* that creativity can take.

Abstract and individual, unique within each and every moment, true creativity, in and of itself, is something much more difficult to define. Any action that flows out from the place within us that exists above the level of the subconscious mind is an expression of true creativity. While anything produced below the dividing line between the heart and the mind, that is based on subconscious programming, is merely a reaction or reproduction. This causes our life to become a re-run program as we repeat the same actions, behavior and thoughts again and again.

Choosing to be creative simply means that we consciously allow ourselves to move beyond the repetitive, habitual programming that normally runs our lives. We are letting go of the way that things have always been in order to provide the conditions that allow the current moment to unfold in a unique, authentic way.

Can you see how it can be helpful to embrace the true meaning of creativity in your own life, especially when it comes to our quest for true happiness?

The truly creative person will see an opportunity in the moment. They will acknowledge the choice that *is* present and will know that he or she can *create* a new experience in an authentic manner, rather than simply reacting in a habitual limited way.

Redefining Choice

Have you ever said to yourself, "I just don't have a choice," or, "I wish that I had a choice"? Both of these despairing statements indicate a belief in a lack of resources and possibility. In other words, you were saying to the world that you did not have what you need in your life and by doing so you were in effect creating your truth through this belief.

How many times have you heard other people say the same two phrases above and you, as an outsider, detached from the emotional charge of the other people's problems, wondered how they could possibly be saying this. From your standpoint you could clearly see a number of options that these individuals had available to them, even though they could not see the same.

Too close to the problem...

This is a statement that accurately describes what is happening in the cases mentioned above. When we are *attached* to the outcome of a situation, we become tied up in the emotional charge of it. Remember the Amygdala, the fear center in the brain that sets us into the fight, flight or freeze experience when triggered by discomfort? This is a perfect example of what can happen when it is set off. The emotional charge of the situation causes a cascade of tension, fear and resistance to occur. As this happens, the individual becomes cut off from the area of the mind and brain where creative solutions exist. As a bystander, without the attachment and fear caused by the triggering of the Amygdala, we are able to retain our connection with our creative resources. This allows us to easily recognize many solutions to the problem that the others, who are suffering the effects of the Amygdala, cannot see. Understanding the way this works can be very helpful, not only when it comes to overcoming challenges, but also in the process of accessing happiness and inner peace.

The truth is, we *always* have a choice in some way. At times, however, these choices may not always be obvious or desirable. They may not seem like much of a choice at all if the resulting effect would produce the experience of pain or grief. Still, whether or not we choose to act on this opportunity, it is important to acknowledge that desirable or not it is still a choice we *do* have, regardless of the perceived outcome. This is important to acknowledge at all times. By doing so, we can greatly reduce, or even remove, resistance from the current moment.

Knowing that we ARE in fact choosing what we are experiencing helps us to feel empowered to a certain degree. It reduces the experience of the victim mentality and places us in the driver's seat of life. In this way we reduce resistance and tension, which allows us to relax and just be. As we've seen earlier, it is in the state of relaxation that opportunity, choice and possibilities present themselves to us naturally and with ease. In other words, we open up the doors for something better to occur by accepting what *is* and taking responsibility for our life and our choices.

By acknowledging that *it is possible* to move from a place of absolute limitation into that of choice in any way is powerful when it comes to choosing happiness on a day-to-day, or moment-to-moment basis. This practice shows us that it is not necessary for things to be perfect in order for us to feel empowered. And even though our day may be filled with rain, we can imagine the blue sky and warmth of the sun on our face. We can choose to smile and dance in the rain... or not. The latter option is an equally powerful choice in every way.

Redefining Addiction and Self-Sabotage

Imagine for a moment that you have decided to *choose* to give this alternate way of thinking a go. You are practicing the art of relaxation, focusing on the essence of what you truly want, aligning your values and beliefs with your dreams and detaching from the emotional charge of the challenges you may be facing. You are opening your heart and mind in a way that allows you to trust that this *can* work for you, and yet you continue to come up with nada, zip, zilch, naught, no happiness, no success, and no inner peace, just more and more misery! At this point you say to yourself...

"What the *BLEEP*? Why isn't this turning out the way Pam said it would? What am I doing wrong? Why isn't this working for me?"

First of all, remember the power contained in the questions you choose to ask. If you want positive help, it is necessary to ask in a positive, proactive way. But aside from this point...

Are you ready for a real eye opener?

You, like many others, may actually be addicted to feeling lousy!

This my friend is called self-sabotage and it is more common than you might think.

For the most part, this experience or addiction affects three of the most important areas of our lives:

- Relationships

- Finances

- Health

Have you ever experienced a situation similar to this…

You get a lucky financial break in some way. It might have been a raise at work, or perhaps you won the lottery or inherited some money, but then all of a sudden you started to experience trouble in your relationships or maybe you gained a significant amount of weight or your health took a turn for the worse in some way. Then after some focus on the relationship, weight or health issue and some improvement in this area of your life, all of a sudden something else comes up, like an unexpected bill, an accident or some other dramatic event that negatively affected another one of the three main areas listed above. At this point, did you think to yourself, "Good grief! Murphy's Law strikes again!"

I don't mean to rob you of your scapegoat or burst your bubble of belief, but the truth is, Murphy didn't do anything! This was simply an effect caused by your own addictive subconscious programming. Once again I must reiterate, that you are not alone in this experience. It happens to nearly everyone on the face of this earth in some way, at some time, and to varying degrees.

So please don't let this news discourage you. In fact, I hope you allow this **awareness** to **empower** you instead!

As mentioned earlier, you cannot fix something when you do not know that it's broken, and in the same way, you cannot create a shift in your subconscious programming until you realize what is truly happening.

When it comes right down to it, our subconscious programming is responsible for creating the foundation for our addictions. In the case of self-sabotage, we are speaking about the addiction to disappointment, or feeling lousy. Now, it would seem that disappointment does not provide any obvious reward. It certainly is not the same as an addiction to binging on sweets or compulsive shopping, even though all three result in us feeling lousy. But the truth is the addiction to disappointment has little to do with the external situation, but rather it is an addiction to the comfort brought on by the chemical release that our bodies create when we engage in, and get wrapped up in the state of drama, no matter what form that drama may take.

This drama is not what any of us would consciously *choose* for ourselves. I personally do not know anyone who sets out in the morning wondering, "How can I mess myself up today?"

What is really happening is an unconscious *reaction* that results when we move too far out of our comfort zone of *familiar* discomfort. Of course, you know what happens when this occurs... the Amygdala is triggered. As an effect, in our closed off state, we react accordingly based on fear and negative memory and subconscious programming. This reaction in turn results in a release of adrenaline and endorphins along with a cascade of other chemicals and hormones that immediately floods our bodies.

...and like a rat in a maze, we once again find ourselves being rewarded amply for successfully following the designated path to the cheese. This reward process occurs for us, no matter how uncomfortable the path we have taken may be.

Even though self-sabotage is an unconscious process that appears to happen beyond our control, it is in fact a process that can be overcome with the right level of awareness, intention, frame of mind and proper techniques. This is where Kaizen small steps and small questions can certainly come in handy!

Imagine what you might do differently now that you know what can occur on a subconscious level, when that bonus comes in at work, or when your love life all of a sudden reaches a new level of satisfaction. Through this new level of understanding and awareness you might all of a sudden find yourself paying closer attention to those impulses begging you to *react* in ways that might damage other areas of your life. This awareness however, is only a beginning. You will have to continue to pay attention, and when you find yourself feeling compelled to react in a damaging way, you will then have to *choose* to take responsibility for your actions in the moment and make decisions in a different way than you have in the past. This shift from reaction to action is powerful.

Thanks to the focus you have placed on practicing small Kaizen steps and small questions throughout the process of reading this book, you *will* be able to identify new ways to make this experience easier on yourself while avoiding things that might trigger the Amygdala. Remember, one small step that we take is worth far more than all of the intentions that are never acted upon.

This new level of understanding definitely has the potential to create some wonderful, happy successful moments in your life, if you allow this to be.

Creative Exploration

1. How would you personally describe creativity? Where are you being creative in your life?

- Notice the areas in your life where you feel you have the greatest amount of choice.

- Now notice where you feel that you have the least amount of choice.

- How might you shift your way of thinking in order to acknowledge a greater amount of choice in *all* areas of your life?

2. Allow yourself to watch your actions a little more closely for a few days this week. As you do, I invite you to pay particular attention to the following:

- Listen to your inner voice. What words are you saying to yourself?

- What tone of voice are you detecting?

- How do these messages make you feel?

If this inner voice is harsh, critical and/or demanding, allow yourself to lighten it up a little bit by balancing the energy of your inner dialogue with some positive, nurturing self talk.

3. What actions do you notice yourself taking on a repetitive basis? Is this behavior helpful? Do your actions help you to feel successful and happy or are they holding you back, keeping you stuck in a self destructive reactionary state?

Notice your emotions as well. Pay close attention to how you feel throughout the week. Are you feeling positive, relaxed and happy, or are you experiencing negative emotions, such as anger, stress, worry and disappointment more often than not? Are you allowing yourself to let go of drama? Or do you feel compelled to sink into it and participate?

Can you think of one tiny step that you *can* take to do things in a slightly different way today? Is there a simple way you can allow yourself to relax and experience a little bit more happiness and inner peace?

Whatever step you choose, please make sure to make it so small that you are guaranteed to create success. This can be as simple as smiling at yourself in the mirror each morning before you brush your teeth. It really doesn't matter how small the step is. Even the tiniest improvement that you make today will allow you to feel better than you did yesterday.

Note: Once you have completed your small step, be sure to acknowledge your success in some small way. This will help to compound the process in a positive way.

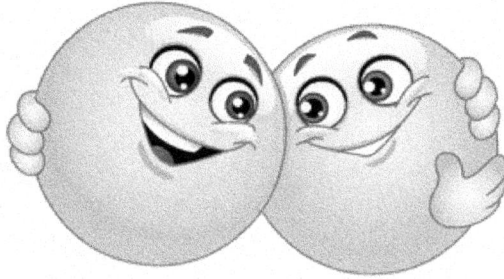

T... TEAM

Some cause happiness wherever they go; others whenever they go.

- Oscar Wilde

Which one are you?

How about the people around you?

Kaizenized Quick Notes

- *If you were meant to go it alone, you would not have been born into a world with over 7 billion other people.*

- *Your team is meant to be unique. It does not need to look like the picture that society has created or deems to be "right." For example: husband, wife, 2.5 kids, with a cat and a dog, bridge club, PTA and a group of friends on the side. The truth is, you get to choose who feels right to connect with along with how many people you want to surround yourself with at any given point in your life.*

- *It is important to protect your dreams by choosing what to share, how much to share, with whom to share this with, and when you will share... if ever. By sharing too much, too soon, with the wrong people, our dreams can be crushed in an instant, causing much unhappiness as a result.*

- *Our team members are often mirrors for us. They reflect the qualities we have in ourselves (both positively and negatively).*

- *Our team quite often brings to our attention some of the possible solutions to the challenges that we may be facing. This is especially helpful when we are just too close to the problem to see things clearly.*

- *Listening to stories of what has worked in the lives of others, as well as challenges that they have faced and overcome, helps us to more deeply understand that we are not so different from each other. It shows us that many people in this world feel the same way that we do. This in turn helps us to feel and know that we are understood. Stories also help to serve as inspiration. They provide a powerful way to share our ideas and techniques.*

- *Our team provides us with an opportunity to both give and receive. Giving automatically opens the doors to happiness, while receiving allows others to feel the same, which in fact makes receiving a form of giving in itself to some degree*

The Extended Version

You've got a friend in me

Humans have always been social beings, creating families, tribes, and other forms of community; we come together to collectively care for our needs. Not only have our personal relationships been helpful through the act of sharing both resources and responsibilities, but our connection with each other has also served to provide us with emotional support as well.

Whether or not we find it easy or difficult to open our hearts and trust, at some point in our lives we all need somebody. Knowing that we are valued, cared for and loved is beneficial for everyone, not only in an emotional sense but also on a physiological level as well. Connecting with others in healthy relationships can reduce stress, while providing support and inspiration. This can often help us to see the good in life in many ways.

The truth is, if we were meant to go it alone, we would not have been born into a world with 7 billion other people. Although we may not find it easy to relate with everyone we meet, there is definitely someone in this world who connects with the way we personally think and understands where we are coming from. These people can see where we are going and can identify what we are presently going through. These are the individuals who make up our team.

Family who are friends and friends who feel more like family: our team is most beneficial when we consciously play a part in choosing who we spend the majority of time with and when. This doesn't mean we will always see eye to eye with every member on our team, but that's ok. In fact, it is often the most difficult relationships that teach us the greatest lessons in life. They provide us with opportunities to learn patience, forgiveness and unconditional love, among other things.

Not all relationships are meant to be difficult though. In this chapter, I would like to focus on the more positive aspects of our own creative support team.

Although no one and no thing outside of ourselves can ever *make* us happy, our team can play a major role in how effective we are in choosing to create a happy, successful life. When we feel that we are understood and supported on our path, it is easier to move though the major challenges and changes in our lives. Simply hearing the words, "I understand. I've been there too," can be more healing than any form of therapy on the market. Finding someone who enjoys the same things that we do, no matter how weird these things may be, has the power to instantly drop our defenses and open our hearts with ease.

Although independence and uniqueness are positive qualities to have, belonging, being a part of something that is bigger than us, and finding similarities with others, can be equally as positive and rewarding. True connection with like-minded individuals can help us to feel strong in our sense of identity. We feel safe knowing that we are not alone on this journey.

The qualities of a healthy support team are the same for most people, with only slight differences depending on what we need personally.

Generally speaking, our closest relationships must meet all of the following needs:

- Provide a sense of belonging
- Validate our self worth
- Ensure a sense of security
- Offer a diverse variety of viewpoints to help us grow as individuals
- Provide a mutual sense of understanding
- Offer an opportunity to both give and receive
- Provide inspiration and support in times of need

Along with the qualities mentioned above, a creative support team of like-minded individuals can help us discover solutions to our problems when we are simply too close to the situation to see clearly. Members of our team have the ability to mirror the qualities that we have in ourselves – both positively and negatively – but, again, are too close to recognize these qualities in ourselves.

By sharing the stories of the challenges we have faced in the past and the ways that we have overcome these challenges, our team can become a source of inspiration while providing helpful techniques in a non- threating, supportive way. Haven't all of the greatest teachers in the world taught through stories and love?

Anyone who inspires us on any level can be part of our team. In fact, it can be healthy to have a variety of people on our team that we connect with in different ways. While some people believe that the Internet and social media are detrimental to our social well-being, I tend to disagree, unless of course this is the only form of social interaction that we engage in. Face to face, in person, online, in a group or one-to-one; no matter how we choose to interact, it is important that we understand that variety is a key to a happy life. It is also helpful to realize that expectations in any relationship are never helpful and love is the foundation upon which all of the greatest relationships are built.

Are your dreams safe?

No matter how close your team is and no matter how safe you may feel, it is important to protect your dreams by choosing what to share, with whom you share it, and when you share it... if ever. By sharing too much, too soon, even amongst the most well meaning people, at the wrong time and in the wrong way, can crush our dreams in an instant.

Here's an example: You just had what *you* believe to be a brilliant idea. You are so excited; every cell in your body feels like it's vibrating. You just can't wait to tell someone, so you look around to see who is the closest to you in that moment of excitement. There you find him or her; your best friend, husband, parent, child, coworker, teacher, or the guy sitting beside you on the bus. While your mind races, and your heart pounds with joy, you pour out your story excitedly, only to be met by a blank stare, or worse yet, a raised eyebrow at the wrong time. In that single moment, you may likely feel as though a knife has struck you in the chest, or that the world has crashed down at your feet. From elation to degradation in a single heartbeat, you are CRUSHED and so is your dream.

The same can happen when the well meaning friend or family member tries to help by telling you all of the ways your idea *might* go wrong. I think most of us have experienced this painful experience at least once in our lives. For some of us, with an overly protective team, it has happened many more times. Even though their intention may be genuinely honorable in their desire to save us from suffering, the pain that we feel as a result of their negative approach hurts just the same. It crushes our enthusiasm and creates a dark shadow that mutes the energy of our dream.

A new idea, a dream, a goal or a profound experience is a fragile thing. It takes nurturing with positive energy to help it grow and thrive. It takes time for us to take it all in, to understand our experience, to process our feelings fully and to allow our creation to be what it will in the best way. Criticism, even the well meaning kind, is like a fist that crushes a tiny sprout as it emerges from the seed. Not a pretty picture is it?

Personally, I sure wish that I would have learned this valuable lesson *much* earlier in my life. It certainly could have saved me from a whole lot of heartache, broken dreams and grief.

Who is on your team?

Your team is meant to be unique. It is meant to meet your own individual needs, whatever they may be. You do not need to fit into the picture that society has created or deems to be "right" for you in any way. For example: a husband, a wife, 2.5 kids, a cat and a dog, bridge club, PTA, with a group of friends on the side. The truth is, YOU get to choose *whom* you spend your time with. You also get to choose *how many* people you want to surround yourself with at any given point in time and *how* you choose to spend your time with them as well.

Today we have far more ways to connect than at any other point in history. You can be isolated, living in the boonies and still be connected in ways that warm your heart and allow you to both give and receive.

Let's get creative!

How would you like to connect and with whom would you like to connect with? The following are some of the many possibilities:

- Groups that focus on a special interest you might have or a hobby you enjoy

- Classes that interest you

- Online groups (just be sure to play safe with your identity)

- The Happiness (R)Evolution in person or online groups *(more about this soon!)*

- Family in the form of friends

- Friends in the form of family

To make things even more interesting, how about adding to our list a group of imaginary friends as well.

(See the creative exploration in this chapter for a fun way to do this.)

Don't forget man's best friend, which, by the way, does not need to be limited to the K9 species. All animals can help us to open our hearts in order to give and receive love, unconditionally.

How about stepping out of your day-to-day routine:

- If you can, why not bring your work to a coffee shop?

- Take a stroll in the park; sit on a bench and people watch or talk with the person sitting next to you... A stranger is just a friend that you haven't met yet.

- You might enjoy attending sports events or concerts just to feel the combined energy of so many people gathered together with a similar interest. I personally love this last one the best. The energy is AMAZING!

There are as many different ways to connect as there are people on the face of this earth and there are just as many, if not more *levels* of connection as well.

Not everyone will be in our "inner circle" but some will. When we allow our life to be enriched by many levels of friendship and connection and we allow those connections to be varied in age, interests, and experience, life begins to take on a wonderful kaleidoscope of experience, bringing with it a new level of beauty in so many ways.

Creative Exploration

1. Notice where you are feeling supported in your life.
Notice where in your life that you might benefit from additional support. Jot down a few notes about this in your journal.

2. What gifts, talents and abilities do you have that might benefit others in your sharing?

3. Imaginary friends are not just for kids. The following exercise can be powerful as well as enjoyable in many ways.

Imagine that you are in your favorite coffee shop, or any other special place where you feel comfortable, relaxed, inspired and connected with other people. Allow yourself to breathe deeply and tune into your creative resources as you see, hear, feel, smell and taste the sensations present in this experience of imagining your special place.

Once you are able to feel yourself present in this scenario, to any degree, allow yourself to focus on the doorway or entrance to your imaginary place.

Notice, one by one, the people walking into your special place: mentors, influential figures, and others who have inspired you in some way. You get to choose who these people are.

For example, if you would like to experience more peace in your life, you might see the Dalai Lama walking in, or perhaps Gandhi might appear instead. If your aim is to feel a greater amount of playful inspiration, you might imagine Dr. Seuss or

Walt Disney, or perhaps one of their characters walking through the door of your special place. For strength and courage, you might discover Nelson Mandela arriving or perhaps your favorite Uncle Fred, who always inspired you to forge ahead.

As each special guest enters, they greet you personally in some special way. As they do, they hand you a folded note containing a special message intended just for you.

As you accept the note, take a moment to look each individual in the eye. Feel the connection of Soul meeting Soul, as the energy of this special meeting moves throughout your body. Avoid the impulse to feel star-struck or in awe. Rather, acknowledge yourself as an equal with these inspirational individuals. The truth is, no matter how much experience you have or have not, you *are* equal to everyone here in this world, as well to all those who have ever been. Each one of us started his or her life as an infant, and we all grew one step at a time. We are all the same in the fact that each of us thrives on love, kindness and connection in our own way.

When you're ready to continue, read the messages that have been given to you. Embrace each one with gratitude and feel yourself connecting even more deeply with your group on a heart to heart level. Feel yourself supported by the combination of experience, resources, energy and capabilities.

Feel free to practice this exercise as often as you like. Make it a personal journey that evolves into something unique.

You might like to meet with your group in various places and in various ways. No matter how you choose to connect with your imaginary team, it is helpful to know that you need only to close your eyes and feel yourself together once again.

I... INDEPENDENCE

"I, not events, have the power to make me happy or unhappy today. I can choose which it shall be.

Yesterday is dead, tomorrow hasn't arrived yet.

I have just one day, today, and I'm going to be happy in it."

-- Groucho Marx

Kaizenized Quick Notes

- *By taking responsibility for our own happiness and basic needs, we release others from these responsibilities, allowing them to feel free to give from the heart rather than from a sense of duty.*

- *Acknowledging our own strengths and desires creates a greater sense of self-confidence and identity*

- *Time alone, combined with self-love, nurturing and self-care, provides the conditions necessary to recharge ourselves in many ways. When we feel recharged and honored by ourselves we naturally experience a sense of gratitude and abundance, which in turn allows us to share our happiness more freely.*

The Extended Version

Who takes care of your needs?

Everyone wants to feel wanted and needed, don't we? When we are wanted for who we are authentically, for our companionship and shared experience, our hearts begin to open and we find ourselves wanting to give even more to the people in our life. The best part about this feeling is that we do so from the heart, rather than from a sense of duty.

Alternatively, when we feel we are wanted only for what we can give, or for what we can do for the other person, we begin to feel used and disrespected. This, in turn, closes the heart and eventually leads to resentment. We may still be giving, but we are certainly not doing so from a place of love, and often because of this, we feel that our own needs are not being met in the process. Over time this scenario can create a downward spiral that sucks the life out of life and limits our happiness and inner peace tremendously.

Not that long ago, little boys were taught that men were supposed to support women financially, while little girls were taught to serve their families. Even though times have changed and we have grown in so many ways, there are still many in our society who continue to feel the damaging effects of this "duty" mentality.

How many of us have given all that we can to others, even to the point of forgetting our own needs? Along with duty, how many of us were raised to believe that it was more benevolent to give than to receive? And how many of us have truly believed this?

Too many!

How about you? How has this been affecting *you*? To tell you the truth, in a personal sense, this state of mind nearly killed me. Thankfully I woke up one day and realized that I deserved my own love and attention just as much as anybody. Hopefully you have realized this too. If not, I strongly suggest you read this chapter at least a few times over, and please be sure to make the most of the creative exploration exercises.

The more that we feel pushed to do something, the less that

most of us want to do anything. Imagine how wonderful it could be to know you are wanted and loved for who you are entirely and that what you give from your heart is appreciated rather than demanded. Sounds like an ideal relationship. Wouldn't you agree?

Of course, this means we would need to take on a greater level of responsibility to meet our own needs while we learn to allow others to be responsible for theirs in a way that works best for them. We would also have to learn to allow ourselves to be whom and what we truly are authentically, without judgment or demand, while we allow others to do the same in their own way.

Let me hear you say, "YAY ME!"

One very small and simple, yet profoundly significant way we can begin to support ourselves and provide for our own needs is by acknowledging the littlest things that we do every day.

Just take a moment to think about how much of your day is spent on the little stuff that never really gets any recognition. I'm talking about things like making your bed, doing the dishes, calling a friend to check in on them, smiling at the grumpy neighbor down the street, controlling your temper (even just a little bit), making a meal, paying your bills, expressing yourself creatively in any way, digging up a weed, washing a window, doing a load of laundry, reading a book, watching a play and enriching your life in a way that makes your heart smile. If you have done even one of the things mentioned above, let me hear you say, **"YAY ME!"**

As you say this, I encourage you to *feel* this expression as a form of true celebration in which you acknowledge your success in every way, no matter how small and insignificant the task you have accomplished may seem. Here's the thing...

When we do NOT acknowledge the little things:

- We often find ourselves wondering what we actually accomplished during the day... feeling that we have done nothing
- We may feel that much of our day has been wasted.
- We may feel that we need to do more.
- Our to-do list grows while our ability to accomplish everything on the list shrinks.

  (How many hours do we think there are in one day?)

- We very often become harder on ourselves , far more demanding and critical of our deeds. This condition places us directly into the painful, damaging state of overwhelm, procrastination, guilt and harsh, critical self-judgment.
- Many of the things that we do get done in a day are accomplished based on the mindset of duty, rather than from a sense of love or caring
- Life is unsatisfying. We feel as though we are never quite good enough, we never accomplish enough, never have enough and never give enough to feel truly worthy.

On the other hand, the more that we DO acknowledge the little things we do in the day, the more meaningful our life becomes.

As Dan Millman, the author of *The Peaceful Warrior* says,

"There are no ordinary moments."

He's right about that, and thankfully we can experience this by simply placing our attention on the little things that fill the hours of our days. By doing so, each moment of our life become a rich, significant experience. Life becomes a celebration!

Some other benefits to acknowledging the little things that we do include:

- Increased self-appreciation along with a sense of true accomplishment
- Shorter to-do lists *(because we realize how much time these little things actually take)*
- With shorter lists, we are better able to create success by completing the things we set out to do in a day. Not only do we gain satisfaction in crossing things off of our list, but also with a reasonable list we often find ourselves crossing ALL of the things off, crumpling up the paper and SLAM DUNKING it in the trash baby!
- We develop a mindset of success, which encourages even more success. By way of simple repetition, success naturally becomes a habit in our lives.
- We look less to outside acknowledgement in order to substantiate our self worth. Instead we simply know that we are worthy.
- Every moment, every action and every task adds to our life, rather than taking time away.
- We find ourselves acknowledging the little things that other people do as well, rather than taking them for granted. This allows everyone to feel more appreciation rather than pressure to do more
- Life is happier. We are far more relaxed. As a result we experience a greater sense of peace and satisfaction.

A little time spent on you is good for everybody

If you're still feeling a little hesitant about spending time on yourself, the following list of benefits to doing so might help you see things in a slightly different way.

- We are better able to rely on our own inner wisdom and intuition to guide the way for us through our lives

- We discover who we are in a deeper sense: what we like, what we do not like, what we need, what we can accept in our lives and what needs to be set free

- We make time for ourselves in a way that does not place demands on another's time or energy

- We enjoy more quiet moments and learn how to relax with greater ease

- Our confidence and self-worth begins to soar

- We resist the impulse to compare ourselves with others

- We find ourselves enjoying our own company.

- We begin to pay closer attention to our senses, both outwardly as well as inwardly, and in doing so we bring a greater depth and dimension to life

- We understand and accept the fact that no one can *make* us feel any particular way unless we choose to allow this

- We find that we are far better able to identify the subconscious programs, beliefs and memories that are affecting our way of thinking in negative ways

- We honor our right to choose. We also honor our right to choose again if desired or necessary. This, in turn, helps us to honor others right to choose as well

- We take responsibility for ourselves, for our thoughts, for our feelings and for our actions. In doing so we empower ourselves

- We understand that we all have everything we need inside ourselves, and that we cannot identify a resource in someone else which is not present within us too. This creates a greater level of trust and respect for all life

- We are better able to celebrate our successes, while we also find it easier to celebrate the successes of others in a genuine way. Competition and comparison cease to complicate our lives.

- We begin to feel complete in our lives as a sense of satisfaction begins to grow. We naturally become happier. We find ourselves finally at peace.

- Life becomes a joy for us and we in turn become a true joy to be around.

"You alone are enough.

You have nothing to prove to anybody."

— Maya Angelou

Of course, I must add that this does not mean that we will never ask for or accept help from anyone. The truth is, we are here to serve each other, not out of a sense of duty, however, but from a loving heart. So instead of giving because we *think* that we *must*, we find ourselves adopting a different mindset, one of gratitude and appreciation and a sincere desire to give with no strings attached. In the long run, everyone is happier, more relaxed and at peace. We are more comfortable asking for what we need and accepting help from others with far more grace and ease. What a wonderful shift from the experience of demanding, waiting, hoping and resenting, or alternatively, feeling unworthy of others' help and thus turning them away.

Creative Exploration

1. List three or more qualities that you love about yourself. What qualities have you heard others say that they admire in you? Can you allow yourself to embrace, and *own* these qualities in a deeper way?

2. Now explore 3 things you might not appreciate in yourself. How can you see these qualities in a more helpful way? For example:

> **Sadness** can help you to develop a greater capacity to feel compassion for other living beings.

> **Anger** has the potential to quickly draw your attention to parts of your life where change needs to take place.

Jealousy indicates an area where you would personally like to/need to place some extra focus and attention in order to grow.

Take care to avoid comparison when using jealousy as an awareness raising tool. Without caution, all of the positive aspects you might gain from this exercise could be easily lost as comparison easily has the power to create discomfort, which of course triggers the Amygdala and places us in the position of procrastination. No positive effect can be experienced in this case. If you *are* finding yourself tempted to compare yourself to another, I encourage you to remember that each one of us is on our own unique journey. Comparison is not only impossible in this sense, considering all of the variables present within our individual lives, but it is also a complete and total waste of time and energy. You are worthy of so much more than this.

3. What do you love to do... have you been doing enough of this lately? Could you do more? Or is there something else that you might like to do in order to nurture yourself?

Where are you meeting your needs? Celebrate this.

At the same time I encourage you to notice where you are relying on others to meet your emotional and physical needs. Is it possible to take back some of this responsibility through self-love and responsibility in a positive, healthy way?

.

"A pessimist sees the difficulty in every opportunity; an optimist sees the opportunity in every difficulty."

Winston S. Churchill

O... OPTIONS & OPPORTUNITIES

"Sometimes your joy is the source of your smile, but sometimes your smile can be the source of your joy."

-- Thich Nhat Hanh

Kaizenized Quick Notes

- *Repetition is the key to creating a strong habit or subconscious program. It is also necessary when we are attempting to change a program or break a habitual state. This applies both positively and negatively*

- *It takes approximately four weeks to establish a habit or routine. In order for the habit to become a natural part of life, it must be maintained through repetition.*

- *Even the greatest tools and techniques are useless if we do not remember to use them on a regular basis. Practicing a technique even when times are good and life is easy will ensure that it will be strong and accessible when we need it most.*

- *Stress and unhappiness can cause us to forget our options. Creating a reminder system, of our most effective techniques and tools, can be helpful in those trying times when the mind is clouded by unhappiness.*

- *New opportunities can potentially cause us to experience discomfort to varying degrees. Fear of the unknown, anticipation of change, and even positive stress can feel overwhelming. New experiences provide us with the perfect opportunity to use Kaizen Small Steps.*

The Extended Version

Repetition is the key

You might recall that we briefly studied the value of repetition in the creative exploration section of chapter 7: Leveraging Success. Here we are once again, revisiting the topic from a different angle in order to keep it fresh, while at the same time elevating our personal understanding. By layering information, we strengthen particular synapses within our brains. In this case we are doing so in order to build a solid foundation in which to access our happiness enhancing techniques, naturally through a habitual state. The truth is, anything can become a habit with a little focus and a lot of repetition. Eating habits, sleeping habits, and spending habits, they're all just activities we repeat again and again and again in a particular fashion until they become a natural part of our lives.

Recall the obstacles chapter for just a moment, specifically the point that explained how thoughts become habitual if we think them repetitively. If the repetitive thoughts we think are negative, we classify them as a problem in the form of a compulsive subconscious program or addiction. Our judgment of this would be based on the fact that these negative thoughts hold us back from experiencing true happiness. Understanding how this works is incredibly helpful for those who wish to live their life in their own way... creatively! What works in a negative sense – creating an addiction that holds us back – also has the power to work in a positive sense as well. Therefore, you can use the same knowledge to break the negative thought pattern and create constructive addictions or habits that have the power to help you experience more happiness in your life. In each case it comes down to this: take care to *choose* thoughts that will help you break down challenges and build positive habits in their place. Remember, this can be done in the easiest, most natural way through small daily steps that build positive momentum and compound naturally.

Imagine how absolutely wonderful it would be to have a habit of success! No matter what you did, you would automatically attract success to yourself. And you would do so naturally with ease. How about the habit of seeing the brighter side of things? In this case without repressing anything, your attention would naturally be drawn to see the opportunities available to you. Your attention would automatically migrate to those positive things that exist in your favor, rather than focusing on the challenges that are getting in your way. How about the habit of relaxed creativity, or experiencing good health, inner peace, meditation, vibrant living or any number of positive, enjoyable habits? Imagine how amazing life could be in this state!

The good news is, this can be done, but only when we choose to focus on our goal in a gentle, progressive way that encourages us to enjoy the process of creating our new habit. Most importantly, this method must be practiced repetitively, taking positive small steps numerous times a day while keeping our focus fresh and ourselves inspired. All of this can occur in small increments of time, lasting minutes or even seconds apiece.

Yes, it's that easy.

It takes approximately one month of daily practice to develop a new habit. It takes about the same to break an old one. In this case you can see that it's really very simple and quick to create positive change. The part that most people find trickiest is simply *remembering* to focus on their goal and practice repetitively throughout the day.

Positive thoughts, relaxing breathing techniques, creative tricks and original ways of thinking can all be helpful in a pinch. But often, once we learn these techniques initially, and we feel that we understand the way they work, we tend to put these tools on a shelf, waiting for the moment when we think we'll need them. We tell ourselves, why use these techniques now if everything is okay? The unfortunate result of this approach, however, is that most often the trick, tool or technique that we've shelved won't work when we really need it. Why? Because we didn't practice it when things were going great. We didn't allow the process to become naturally ingrained, strong and reliable like our other *"bad"* habits that we repeated day after day whether we needed them or not. It would be the same as waiting for "test day" before studying or waiting for the day of the big race before you decided to work out and train. Neither the ingrained knowledge nor strength would be there when it was necessary.

Another thing that often holds us back from practicing our creative techniques on a daily basis is the deep down feeling that small steps are a waste of time.

We, as a society, have gotten so used to the idea of "Go big or go home." This belief has *also* become a habit for many of us. Thankfully it need not be. If we simply remind ourselves on a daily basis that little bits of something that we *do* are worth a whole lot more than planning big and *doing nothing* as we find ourselves procrastinating in the state of overwhelm due to our BIG expectations, eventually we'll begin to see things differently. Then watch out world! You will be amazed at what you can do in tiny increments, especially when the process of taking these small steps, one at a time, improving a little bit each day, becomes a habit in its own right!

In my own experience, the process of Kaizen small steps has been the key to all of my major accomplishments. Its how I created the non profit association Kaizen Inspired Life. It is also how I wrote this book, created each course, and developed every project. Its also how I stopped a thirty year smoking habit, after I'd tried everything else on the market. Without small steps I know, without a doubt that none of these things would have happened. I also know that I would have missed out on SO MANY wonderful things in my life, like the adventures that I experienced other side of the world, travelling on my own, not once but twice. It is also how I managed to buy and furnish the home that I currently live in. Even though the steps may be small, I guarantee… the results are often utterly amazing.

Drawing a blank? How's your plan B, C, D… and Z?

When times are challenging, it is common for us to develop a type of amnesia. Even the most familiar techniques that we have been practicing on a regular basis can be difficult to remember when the Amygdala shuts down the parts of our brain responsible for conscious thought and positive memory. In these moments we often find ourselves blanking out and forgetting what has worked for us in the past to overcome challenges similar to the ones that we are facing today. We forget our options. We forget what works. In the worst case scenario, when we are feeling the weakest, we might often feel we have no options at all. However, once we have an opportunity to relax and reconnect with the creative part of ourselves, we wonder how we could have forgotten such important things! That's what happens in the land of the Amygdala. And the truth is... It happens to everybody.

Thankfully, there is a simple way to work around this problem by creating a contingency plan. If we take a moment, now and then, during the times when we are feeling relaxed and creative, to plan ahead for stressful experiences, we can easily outsmart the Amygdala with plans b, c, d... and z!

By writing down a list of things that have worked for us in the past, including techniques and activities that help us to relax and tap into our creative resources, along with things that bring us joy and happiness, we create a way to remember these helpful things when times are challenging.

In a sense, our list is similar to a menu in a restaurant. When you're really hungry for happiness and just too tired to cook it up from scratch. You can look at the menu, and remember what helped to satisfy your hunger for joy in the past. Then before you know it your order is up and you have what you crave... easy as pie and just as delicious!

Sometimes it's best to just call it a day

Now, what about those times when life just feels far too difficult in every conceivable way? No matter what you do, you just cannot seem to relax to any degree. You're tired and your contingency plan, no matter how well it has been developed, is being met with a load of resistance? What then? At this point my friend, it is time to simply take a break.

No matter how much we've grown or how proficient we've become in the art of choosing happiness, it is always possible for a new level of challenge to meet us in a way that takes our breath away. Just knowing this can happen, however, will make it a little easier to move through the experience when it happens. A death in the family, a serious illness, a devastating event, major hormonal shifts, divorce, moving house or any other serious life change can knock even the strongest, happiest people off their feet and onto their seat. This is just part of the human condition, and it's okay.

During difficult moments the most important thing to remember is that we are not alone. Others have been in this place too. And even though we may not be able to make the situation better, there are some things that we can do.

The following is a list of suggestions that you might find helpful during especially challenging times. Please feel free to add them to your contingency plan.

1. Stop pushing so hard. It's getting you nowhere fast. In fact, the act of pushing could actually be spiraling you deeper into negativity. The solution? Let go and breathe. You might like to re-read chapter 3 in this book -- RELAXING.
2. Get yourself some rest. Have a sleep. Fatigue has a way of preventing us from seeing clearly while it knocks us out of balance emotionally. Thankfully, the opposite is true. A good night's sleep can help us to see much clearer in the morning.
3. Drink some water. Dehydration can have the same effect on us as a lack of sleep. Proper hydration is vital to good health, balanced emotions and clear thinking.
4. Call a friend and cry if you need to. Just let it out. Bottling

up thoughts and emotions helps no one. Once you have gotten it out of your system, take care not to dwell on your story by repeating it again and again. This too can become an addiction if not watched carefully.

5. Eat a healthy meal. Too much junk food can mess with your emotions by causing imbalances in hormone and blood sugar levels. This imbalance in itself can absolutely wreak havoc on your mental and emotional state.

6. Go for a walk. Fresh air and exercise not only has the power to release a flood of *feel good* endorphins into your blood stream, but it also has the ability to clear the mind and make the body feel great.

7. Meditate, listen to music that fills your heart with peace and happiness, take a warm bath or hot shower, make a cup of relaxing tea, spray lavender on your pillow, or do anything else that helps you to slow down your heart rate and ease into the moment of now with a little more peace and ease.

8. Remind yourself that this too shall pass, and know that it most certainly will. If you allow yourself to remember that you have successfully made it through ALL of the other challenges in your life. You WILL make it through this one too.

9. If you find that none of the above is working for you and you just cannot escape from this dark place, it may be time to seek professional help. This is not to be seen as a failure or a weakness in any way. In fact it is an admirable quality to be willing to take responsibility for your own state of well being by keeping an open mind with respect to *all* of the helpful resources that are available.

Creative Exploration

1. Take a moment to quickly jot down a few things that have stood out in this book for you. What points have hit home the most? What touched you in the deepest way? What did you find helpful and what do you think you might be able to use in the future to create a greater experience of happiness, true success and inner peace in your life?

2. Remember that reminders are an important part of the journey. When challenges strike and the Amygdala is triggered, what do you think might help you to quickly and easily remember these things that have worked in in this process so that you can use them again?

As you create your own unique reminders, remember that it is helpful to include as many of your senses as possible. By doing so, you increase your ability to open the channel to your creative subconscious with far greater ease.

3. It can be helpful to write down the list of tools and techniques that your are particularly drawn to that specifically apply to all 10 major areas of the HAPPINESS (R)EVOLUTION process.

RELAXATION – Write down a few techniques that you find helpful when it comes to releasing the hold that the Amygdala has on you while tapping into your creative resources once again.

ESSENCE - Create a unique reminder of the quality of energy you wish to feel. It can be helpful to do this in a unique way that helps you to feel the essence. For example, you may want to find a special quote or a poem that expresses the quality of the essence you want to feel. Collage a picture that visually expresses this powerful energy. Find a song that sums up your feelings, or write your own prose. Pour your feelings out on the page. Whatever you use, make sure that you can feel the energy of the essence when you visit your reminder again.

VALUES – What beliefs do you hold that *support* your dream? Write them down.

OBSTACLES - Create a reminder of how powerful it can be to experience life one moment at a time. How can you see into your situation more clearly? What techniques help you to shift your focus from the victim mentality of why this challenge is happening *to* you and instead, experiencing the empowered creative state of why this is happening *for* you.

LEVERAGING SUCCESS - What does success mean to you personally? What does happiness feel like?

Suggestion: Write, paint, collage or create any form of reminder that expresses the feeling of energy in these particular states along with any corresponding tools or techniques that help you to experience this feeling.

UNDERSTANDING - Remind yourself of the true meaning of creativity, choice and subconscious addiction in a way that helps you to gain a greater sense of clarity in your own life and experiences.

TEAM – Create a list of friends you can call upon when you need support and understanding. Then write a list of places where you can tap into the energy of others in a general way, in order to feel supported and inspired in the way you need. (i.e.: a group event, museum, gallery, coffee shop or any place where the energy feels inspiring to you.)

INDEPENDENCE – Create a list of the special things you love to do for yourself along with the important things that you can do for yourself in order to support yourself on your own journey.

OPTIONS AND OPPORTUNITIES – What specific tools or techniques have been helpful for you in general? Write a list of all that apply. Keep the list running and add to it when you can.

You may also like to create a running list of all the things that you would like to try in your life... some call it a bucket list. Not only can this list help you to remember the things that are important to you, but it also has the power to attract the energy and conditions that can make these things possible. One more benefit to this process is that by writing your dreams down on paper, you no longer have to waste energy by holding them all in your head.

NEXT STEPS – Take them, no matter how small they may be. Reading is a good start, but action, even the tiniest bit, is more powerful than anything.

"If you keep on saying a single thing to yourself, you are likely to attract it to yourself, dreaming it always, then in a twinkle of an eye, it comes to you."

Michael Bassey Johnson

$\mathcal{N}$... NEXT STEPS

"*Twenty years from now you will be more disappointed by the things that you didn't do than by the ones you did do. So throw off the bowlines. Sail away from the safe harbor.*

Catch the trade winds in your sails.

Explore. Dream. Discover."

- *H. Jackson Brown Jr.*

Kaizenized Quick Notes

- *We can move forward. We can move backward but we can never stay the same. We do not need to take giant leaps in order to create forward propulsion in our lives. Small steps, that we take on a daily basis, are all we really need.*

- *Even the tiniest step taken toward your dream, each day, will move you forward much quicker than all of the dreams that you never acted upon.*

- *What have you always wanted to do that you haven't done yet? By exploring what you dreamed of as a young child, you can begin to prime your creative imagination today and by doing so, you will gain a greater sense of clarity and vision in every way.*

- *What has worked the most for you in this process? What was your favorite part of the book? How can you make the exercises work even better for yourself personally? What steps can you take?*

- *How can you share this information and inspiration with others? Remember that by giving we will always receive!*

The Extended Version

Even positive changes can be scary.

That's ok.

So here we are, nearing the end of this book. I hope by now you're feeling inspired in a relaxed, creative way. I also hope that you have been taking advantage of this creative process by experimenting with the tools and techniques while increasing your awareness, and as a result experiencing positive change in many wonderful ways.

Now, I would like to ask: how might you take what you've learned one step further on your own unique journey? How might you put this information and these techniques into practice on a *regular* basis rather than just experiencing it as a temporary thing? Remember, Kaizen small steps are a great way to begin creating momentum in an easy and natural way. By doing so you will effectively avoid pulling the trigger on the Amygdala in a way that results in self defeating overwhelm.

Gentleness and a steady pace really does pay off in the long run. Remember the story of the tortoise and the hare?

A dream without action is cause for heartbreak

What have you always felt drawn to do, or have been curious about doing for some time now? Have you ever dreamed of playing the guitar or another musical instrument? When you were little, did you want to grow up to become a dancer, but as time went on you decided that you were just too old or too busy to try? How about photography, painting or writing the next best selling novel? What has been holding you back from taking a step toward fulfilling these dreams? Perhaps a Kaizen small step or small question might be exactly what you need to pull your dream out of the closet, dust off the cobwebs and give it a go. Seriously, what are you waiting for? You have nothing to lose when you take small steps, and absolutely everything to gain!

The truth is there will never be a "right" time or a "perfect" time for anything. In fact, if you are waiting for that perfect time, you might as well let go of your dream right here and now. Stop jerking yourself around and playing with your own heart strings. There will never will be a perfect time. It simply does not exist.

What do you think? Do you believe this? Or perhaps could you be holding onto the perfect time theory in order to protect yourself from losing your dream should something fall out of place? People often never try to fulfill their dreams in the fear that they may fail and so they wait for the BEST, most opportune moment in order to provide themselves with the greatest chance of succeeding. But this, is merely an avoidance technique. There is no better time than the present, and if you proceed with small steps – at least to start – you might surprise yourself in the most wonderful ways.

For over 30 years I too had a dream that I kept in the closet. Afraid of judgment and negative comments, I kept my dream to myself and shared it with nobody. From the time I was a very young child, I dreamed of being a painter. For more than three decades I imagined myself standing in front of an easel, creating beautiful masterpieces and selling them in a gallery. All those years, fear of failure and ridicule kept me from pursuing that dream. I told myself that only "talented" people with proper training and skill could do such a thing. I believed that I did *not* have that talent. I did *not* have the skill and I did *not* have the training. Regardless of my beliefs, I continued to dream until one day it became far too painful to allow this vision to remain dormant, and so I took my first baby steps toward making my dream a reality. I bought a set of watercolor pencils and a year and a half later, those small steps added up to something quite amazing! I held my first solo show in a local gallery and sold over two thousand dollars in paintings! Since then I have continued to sell my art independently online and occasionally in person.

By the artist dream did not stop there. A few years ago, I also took up photography, which too had been a long standing dream. I have since sold many pieces in this medium as well. The interesting part of all this is that I never did receive any formal training. Rather, I simply followed my heart and allowed the art to flow through me in the way it wanted to.

Creating in this way began to take on the qualities of a dance between myself and the pure creative spirit. I listened to the inner nudges and the art created itself through me. As a result of listening and creating, this process resulted not only in art but also in the form of a technique that I have since shared with many others in a popular workshop called, "The Art of Spiritual Painting." By sharing this creative dance, many more people have also had the opportunity to experience the joy of creating art from the heart and in the process have amazed themselves at what they were able to create! So you see, there is always another step on the journey of happiness, and there is always a way to turn our dreams into reality if we are willing to allow this to happen, by taking the first step on the journey of a lifetime.

Prepare for the dam to break!

Perhaps you might be having a little trouble coming up with ideas of things that you would like to try, things that you might like learn or steps that you'd like to take. That's ok. Sometimes it can take a little while to begin siphoning water from the creative well. But let me forewarn you, when the ideas do start to come through, be ready and be prepared for the dam to break! You could very well become flooded by an incredible amount of ideas, so many ideas in fact, that this too can be cause for overwhelm! There *is* a way to prepare for this, though. The trick is to simply write down your ideas as they come to you and play with the ones that touch your heart in the deepest way.

Maintaining your creative journal can provide you with an outlet in which to explore these dreams. Writing is a wonderful way to stay focused and balanced, while experimenting with the pure joy of creating.

Creative Exploration

1. Think back to your early childhood days. Can you remember what you wanted to be when you grew up?

...a firefighter, forest ranger, ballerina, policeman, doctor, teacher, astronaut, circus clown, or something else?

These too were merely symbols for a deeper desire.

In the quest for true happiness, it can be helpful to look back to the earlier times and experiences in our lives; specifically to our childhood activities, dreams and desires. The reason being that these actions and ideas reflected who and what we truly were before we allowed ourselves to become that which the world thought we should be.

When we look to the essence of the dreams we had as a child and the activities we loved to engage in, we can discover many interesting and helpful bits of information that we can use right now to create more happiness, true success and inner peace in our lives today. Even though it is true that we have changed in *many* ways since we were young, it is also true that deep down inside ourselves, that little kid still exists and our *essential* needs are still there. They have stayed the same.

For example, if you wanted to be a firefighter, you may have been expressing your authentic sense of identity and purpose along with the need for the following qualities in your life:

- A deep love for life and the need to preserve it at all cost
- A sense of protectiveness for your fellow human beings
- A need for adventure and excitement
- A desire for variety and movement
- A sense of belonging to a worthy cause and a part of a valuable team

If a life lived as a forest ranger was your childhood dream, the following qualities may reflect your deeper desires:

- A profound connection with life and nature in a way that

replenishes and recharges you

- A need for freedom, open space and fresh air
- The opportunity to challenge yourself
- Adventure and serenity
- A sense of balance; of all things in order, just as it is in nature

If you wanted to be a ballerina, you may find yourself identifying with the following:

- The need for beauty and strength in your life
- A desire for balance and precision
- A yearning to add to the enjoyment of life through entertainment and skillful technique

Of course, this is only a brief list of qualities associated with each career.

What do *you* believe might have been the deeper desire behind your own childhood dreams? What qualities do you currently possess that support such a dream? As you answer these questions, be sure to look beyond the obvious, into the *essence* of what each career represents. You can do this by asking yourself what it might *feel* like to do such work. If you cannot remember what you wanted to be as a child or if you recall that you could never decide on any one particular career, perhaps you might describe yourself as a seeker, a student of the world, a lover of life? Is it possible that even back then you would not allow yourself to be placed in a box or classified and judged in any way?

In its own way, NOT choosing IS choosing. It is choosing not to choose. It is allowing yourself to be open while you allow life to unfold in its own way. What qualities do you feel are contained in this way of thinking and feeling?

2. The exercise above is not limited to the dreams you had as a child. In fact, it can be in your best interest to look at both ends of the spectrum or timeline:

- Where you were back then
- Where you are today

By doing so you can achieve a much clearer picture of the essences that you feel you need in your life in order to truly experience happiness. So now I invite you to look a little deeper into your desires once again. If you could have *any* job in the world right now today, (and miraculously you would instantly be qualified for it) what would you choose?

It can be helpful to ask yourself the following question as you explore this exercise…

What makes your heart beat faster?

What makes time fly?

What has the power to take your breath away?

Once you discover what you are secretly, or not so secretly longing for, you might like to ask yourself this:

Right here and now, what is one small micro step that I can take in order to experience the essence of my dream today?

Let's use the firefighter dream as an example. If you have a deep love for life and the need to preserve it at all cost, what might you do today in order to satisfy this essential need?

- Is there a cause that you could volunteer for, one that helps to accomplish this goal?

- Would the act of donating money satisfy you or would you need to donate your time and energy in order to meet this need?

Now let's take a look at the need for adventure and excitement as well as a desire for variety and movement. How do you think you might be able to satisfy this need (even a tiny bit) today?

- Perhaps there is a hobby that you have been interested in, that you've been putting off? Could it be time to take a small step in this direction? This step could be as simple as daydreaming about the activity or looking it up on your computer.

What else do you think might work for you?

When we finally allow ourselves to accept the fact that nothing in this life is as it appears to be, that everything we see, hear, feel, smell, taste and sense in *any way* is merely a symbol for something deeper, then we will have finally reached the pivotal point of acknowledging *truth* in our lives. We will finally begin to LIVE rather than merely existing based on subconscious programming. Only then will we become aware of the infinite possibilities and opportunities that exist all around us in every moment. Only then can we begin to create our experiences in the way that we *choose*, while allowing room for miracles to show up in ways that exceed even our greatest and grandest dreams.

Relaxed awareness, conscious choice, creativity and allowing the best to be... now that's what I'm talkin' about! That my friend is the recipe for true happiness, authentic success and lasting inner peace.

Here you have it in your hand; time to get cooking!

Enjoy!

A man is not rightly conditioned until he is a happy, healthy, and prosperous being; and happiness, health, and prosperity are the result of a harmonious adjustment of the inner with the outer of the man with his surroundings.

James Allen

THE HAPPINESS (R)EVOLUTION

"It was only a sunny smile, and little it cost in the giving, but like morning light it scattered the night and made the day worth living."

- F. Scott Fitzgerald

The best way to multiply your happiness is to share it with others!

Happiness is contagious... Pass it on!

For more than fifteen years I have studied the subconscious mind, addictions and creativity. In the process I have been blessed with the discovery of many wonderful tools and techniques that have helped me to personally tap into an incredible depth of happiness and inner peace. The effect of this experience was also a gift in that it resulted in a greater ability to overcome limitations and challenges in an easy, natural and enjoyable way. Of course when something this good happens in our lives we cannot help feeling the need to share it with everybody! But how to do this in the most effective way? It would take a book of more than ten thousand pages to share all that I have learned with you.

But seriously, who would want to read a book that big when it's more fun to put these techniques into practice experientially?

So instead of writing a book of monstrous proportion, I have created something even greater to offer to you. This creation is a unique opportunity to continue the happiness journey in a supportive environment, with like-minded individuals through the HAPPINESS (R)EVOLUTION in-person and online groups!

Wondering why the R is in brackets?

Rather than a **R**ebellious, **R**esistant, up**R**ising...

The HAPPINESS (R)EVOLUTION is an **EVOLUTION**ary process that EMPOWERS PEOPLE with the art of deep **R**ELAXATION and CREATIVITY.

Through increased awareness and creative techniques, you can **R**ELEASE yourself from the limitations that may be holding you back from experiencing lasting happiness in your life. In this place of reduced resistance, **R**ESPECT for self and others naturally develops and grows to the point where you find yourself able to take **R**ESPONSIBILITY for your own state of happiness through conscious creative choice.

What can you do with the HAPPINESS (R)EVOLUTION?

- Join an in-person meet-up group where available. To find a group near you, please visit: http://www.meetup.com/Kaizen-Inspired-Life.

- Participate online and via teleconference. You can start by claiming your HAPPINESS (R)EVOLUTION Starter Kit. Further information can be found in the sidebar here: http://kaizeninspiredlife.com/happiness-revolution/

- Join the Facebook HAPPINESS (R)EVOLUTION group page for daily inspiration and an opportunity to share more of what makes you happy. https://www.facebook.com/groups/TheHappinessREvolution/

- Become a supporting member of Kaizen Inspired Life – Creative Training and Outreach Association in order to make sure you are the first to hear of ALL the great programs that continue to sprout from the branch of the HAPPINESS (R)EVOLUTION. Visit our website at: http://kaizeninspiredlife.com/ to find out more.

- Train to become a Kaizen Creative NLP facilitator and start a HAPPINESS (R)EVOLUTION group in your own area. Visit: http://kaizeninspiredlife.com/training/ for more info

As you well know whatever you give, you will also receive. So why not share a little happiness today?

Here are some simple ways that you can share the HAPPINESS (R)EVOLUTION and help to make the world a HAPPIER place for yourself and others:

- Donate to Kaizen Inspired Life's mission by visiting our website -- Every dollar makes a difference.
- Volunteer your special skills, talents and abilities to help Kaizen Inspired Life's cause
- Happiness is contagious, so pass it on! Share it freely!
- Tell your friends and family about this book and about the HAPPINESS (R)EVOLUTION.
Buy them a copy if you can. It makes a wonderful gift.
- Add as many people to the HAPPINESS (R)EVOLUTION Facebook group as you would like..
- Check out our website (KaizenInspiredlLife.com) and pick up some **Pay it Forward Happiness Hint cards.** Pass them out randomly.
- Get yourself a HAPPINESS (R)EVOLUTION reminder wristband while you visit our site. Take advantage of this great way to remember your happiness intention by catching your attention each time you see the band on your wrist.

There are no limits to the way you can share happiness.

What else might work for you?

Your time is limited, so don't waste it living someone else's life. Don't be trapped by dogma - which is living with the results of other people's thinking. Don't let the noise of others' opinions drown out your own inner voice. And most important, have the courage to follow your heart and intuition.

Steve Jobs

ABOUT THE AUTHOR

Pam Ellis earned her Ph.D. in philosophy, specializing in holistic counseling in 2014.

She is the founder, executive director and senior instructor of Kaizen Inspired Life – Creative Training and Outreach Association, a registered federal non-profit. Pam is also the creator of Kaizen Creative NLP and the powerful E.V.O.L.V.E. method of creative life coaching.

Since 1998 she has helped thousands of people to discover a greater sense of happiness, inner peace and purpose in their lives.

As an instructor, therapist, artist, author and mother of three, Pam understands the art of living life wholeheartedly through the art of small steps and progressive change.

She specializes in the areas of:

- Authentic creativity
- Kaizen philosophy
- Holistic counseling, with an emphasis in subconscious addiction therapy
- Meditation and mindfulness
- Energy therapy

Pam believes that we were not put on this earth to suffer in needless ways, but rather we are meant to rise up and live our lives richly while taking steps to turn our dreams into reality.

ALSO FROM KAIZEN INSPIRED LIFE

- *The HAPPINESS (R)EVOLUTION* – Your hands-on creative guide for eliciting true happiness, authentic success and a lasting sense of peace... from the inside.

- Kaizen Creative NLP Practitioner Certification Program

- *Modern-Day Meditation* – A No-Cushion-Necessary Experiential Guide to deep relaxation and increased awareness... simplified

- *The Art of Spiritual Painting* – Releasing the flow of creative inspiration and intuition in your own life

- *In Living Color* – The Art of Living ... Creatively

Coming soon: Self-paced study programs

- *The HAPPINESS (R)EVOLUTION multimedia Udemy course*

- *Kaizen Creative NLP for personal and professional use*

- *E.V.O.L.V.E. coaching certification program.*

For more information visit

http://KaizenInspiredLife.com